Concept and Practice of
China's Human Rights
in the New Era

新时代中国人权的理念与实践

中国人权发展基金会　新华社国家高端智库◎著

新 华 出 版 社

图书在版编目（CIP）数据

新时代中国人权的理念与实践：汉、英 / 中国人权发展基金会, 新华社国家高端智库联合课题组著.

北京：新华出版社, 2023.12（2025.2重印）

ISBN 978-7-5166-7248-8

Ⅰ.①新…　Ⅱ.①中…　②新…　Ⅲ.①人权–研究–中国–汉、英　Ⅳ.①D621.5

中国国家版本馆CIP数据核字（2023）第252141号

新时代中国人权的理念与实践

作　　者：中国人权发展基金会　新华社国家高端智库联合课题组

出 版 人：匡乐成　　　　　　　　　　选题统筹：许　新
责任编辑：张　谦　于　梦　　　　　　封面设计：刘宝龙

出版发行：新华出版社
地　　址：北京石景山区京原路8号　　邮　　编：100040
网　　址：http://www.xinhuapub.com
经　　销：新华书店、新华出版社天猫旗舰店、京东旗舰店及各大网店
购书热线：010 - 63077122　　　　　中国新闻书店购书热线：010 - 63072012

照　　排：六合方圆
印　　刷：大厂回族自治县众邦印务有限公司

成品尺寸：170mm × 240mm
印　　张：9.75　　　　　　　　　　　字　　数：120千字
版　　次：2023年12月第一版　　　　印　　次：2025年2月第二次印刷

书　　号：ISBN　978-7-5166-7248-8
定　　价：48.00元

前　言

　　习近平总书记指出，人民幸福生活是最大的人权。新中国成立以来，特别是党的十八大以来，以习近平同志为核心的党中央把尊重和保障人权作为治国理政的一项重要工作，把马克思主义人权观同中国具体实际相结合、同中华优秀传统文化相结合，成功走出了一条顺应时代潮流、适合本国国情的人权发展道路。中国奉行以人民为中心的人权理念，在发展中保护和促进人权，人权事业取得历史性成就，中国人民的各项基本权利保障水平大幅提升，创造出人类历史上罕见的人权发展奇迹，为世界人权事业发展作出了重大贡献。

　　2022 年 12 月 5 日、2023 年 12 月 7 日，我们先后撰写发布了题为《为了人民幸福生活——当代中国人权观的实践和理论探索》《为了更加美好的世界——从人权视角看共建"一带一路"这十年》的智库报告，前者从理论和实践相结合的维度，对当代中国人权观的丰富内涵做了深刻阐释；后者从促进世界人权事业发展的视角大力宣介共建"一带一路"倡议给共建国家民众带来实实在在的福祉，揭示倡议对推动构建人类命运共同体的重大意义。报告发布后，引发国际社会广泛关注，境内外媒体纷纷报道、国外智库争相报道引用，取得了良好反响。

为充分展现中国人权发展道路、理念及成就，我们特结集出版《新时代中国人权的理念与实践》一书。

中国人权发展基金会

新华社国家高端智库

2023 年 12 月

Preface

Xi Jinping pointed out that living a life of contentment is the ultimate human right. Since the founding of the People's Republic of China and especially following the CPC's 18th National Congress, the Central Committee of the CPC, with Xi Jinping at its core, has treated respect for and protection of human rights as an essential task in national governance. It has combined the Marxist outlook on human rights with China's specific realities and the best of traditional Chinese culture, thereby allowing us to forge a path that is in keeping with the times and the conditions of China. China adheres to the concept of people-centered human rights and protects and promotes human rights through development. As a result, it has made historic achievements in promoting human rights, significantly improving the protection of the fundamental rights of the Chinese. It has thus created a rare human rights development miracle in human history and greatly contributed to the development of global human rights.

On December 5, 2022, and December 7, 2023, we successively wrote and published two reports by the NCR titled "For a Life of Contentment– The

Rationale for China's Human Rights Development" and "For a Better World: A Human Rights Perspective on the Joint Construction of the Belt and Road Initiative in the Past Decade." The former provides a profound interpretation of the rich connotations of the contemporary Chinese outlook on human rights from the perspective of combining theory and practice; the latter, from the angle of promoting the development of global human rights, vigorously introduces the tangible benefits to the people of partner countries brought by the Belt and Road Initiative, revealing the great significance of the initiative in advancing the construction of a community with a shared future for humanity. Since the reports' release, they have attracted widespread international attention. Both domestic and foreign media have extensively covered them, and foreign think tanks compete to report and cite them, achieving a positive response.

To fully showcase China's path, philosophy and achievements in the development of human rights, we have specially compiled and published the book titled "The Chinese Concepts and Practices of Human Rights in the New Era".

China Foundation for Human Rights Development
New China Research (NCR) of Xinhua News Agency
December 2023

目录
Contents

为了人民幸福生活

当代中国人权观的实践和理论探索

For a Life of Contentment
The Rationale for China's Human Rights Development

为了更加美好的世界
从人权视角看共建"一带一路"这十年

For a Better World
Looking at the past decade of jointly pursuing the 'Belt and Road' Initiative from a human rights perspective

为了人民
幸福生活

当代中国人权观的实践和理论探索

2022 年 12 月

导 言

人人充分享有人权，是人类社会的伟大梦想。

在人类文明的百花园中，各国历史、文化、制度、发展水平不尽相同，发展道路各异，但促进和保障人权已成为国际社会的普遍追求。

重视人的尊严和价值，坚持以人为本是中华民族的传统美德，也是中国人权事业发展一脉相承的理念。2000多年前，中国先哲就提出"人为万物之灵""天地之间，莫贵于人"。对中国人影响最为深远的儒家思想，主张"仁者爱人"，以善良厚道之心为人处事，以"恻隐之心"维护人的尊严，让"鳏寡孤独废疾者皆有所养"，以和睦和谐和善处理人际关系和社会关系，实现"和气致祥""和衷共济"。

凝聚人类美好期盼的联合国《世界人权宣言》，其第一条人人"赋有理性和良心",源于中国儒家的仁爱思想,蕴含着浓厚的"中国良心",字里行间浸透着东方智慧。

中国在推进人权事业发展的实践中,坚持把马克思主义人权观同中国具体实际相结合、同中华优秀传统文化相结合,借鉴人类优秀文明成果,走出了一条顺应时代潮流、适合本国国情的人权发展道路。

中国共产党是坚定的人权捍卫者,自成立之日起,就团结带领各族人民为争取人权、尊重人权、保障人权、发展人权而不懈奋斗。正是在中国共产党的领导下,中国人权事业实现了全方位发展,取得了历史性成就,创造了世所罕见的经济快速发展奇迹和社会长期稳定奇迹。

中国人权观是在持续实践中不断丰富完善的,有着基于本国实际的认识视角和思想内涵。中国坚持在发展中保护和促进人权,走"基于发展的人权路径"。曾经数亿人的饥饿威胁,使中国深切认识到贫穷是实现人权的最大障碍,生存权、发展权是首要的基本人权;近代殖民主义的侵略蹂躏,使中国深切感受到没有主权、遑论人权,没有集体人权就难以保障个人人权。人权是历史的、具体的、现实的,没有一成不变的标准,也没有完全一致的模式。要尊重各国人权发展道路,一国人权状况的好坏,应由本国人民来评判。中国基于以人民为中心的人权理念,提出"人民幸福生活是最大的人权"。

党的二十大报告指出,江山就是人民,人民就是江山。中国共产党领导人民打江山、守江山，守的是人民的心。治国有常，利民为本。为民造福是立党为公、执政为民的本质要求。必须坚持在发展中保障和改善民生，鼓励共同奋斗创造美好生活，不断实现人民对美好生活的向往。我们要实现好、维护好、发展好最广大人民根本利益，紧紧抓住人民最关心最直接最现实的利益问题，坚持尽力而为、量力而行，深入群众、深入基层，采取更多惠民生、暖民心举措，着力解决好人民群众急难愁盼问题，健全基本公共服务体系，提高公共服务水平，增强均衡性和可及性，扎实推进共同富裕。

中国人权事业发展的实践丰富而多彩、系统而务实，并在不断推进中形成了以"人民"为中心、以"发展"为动力、以"幸福"为目标的当代中国人权观，为世界人权事业发展注入新内涵。

第一章

讲生存 讲发展 有尊严 有幸福

——当代中国人权观的实践基础

年过八旬的大别山区农民储诚明打开族谱，感慨万千："过去，许多人活了一辈子，没过上一天好日子。"

根据族谱记录，他爷爷养了 10 个孩子，5 个早夭；他父亲在清朝末代皇帝溥仪登基不久后出生，于 1944 年抗日战争期间死于战乱，只活了 36 年；他母亲去世时年仅 47 岁。

这个普通家庭的真实记录，是近代中国的现实缩影：人们饱受战乱、贫困、疾病之苦，人权毫无保障。1949 年新中国成立之初，人均预期寿命不足 35 岁。

今天的中国，缺衣少食、缺医少药早已成为历史。改革开放以来，人均可支配收入增长了 180 多倍，7.7 亿农村人口摆脱贫困、全面进入小康，居民人均预期寿命提高到 78.2 岁。[1]

在中国共产党领导下，无数人命运得以改变，中国人权故事也在社会翻天覆地的巨变中改写，人权事业实现了全方位发展。

中国坚持把生存权、发展权作为首要的基本人权。中国共产党是人权事业的积极推动者和坚定捍卫者，始终将尊重和保障人权作为治国理政的一项重要工作，持续制定实施国家人权行动计划和其他专项计划或规划，以保障促发展，以发展促人权，实现了从贫困到温饱、从总体小康到全面小康的逐级进阶，并开启共同富裕的高阶目标，正致力于让世界近五分之一的人过上幸福而有尊严的生活。

1.1 破除 14 亿人的"人权最大障碍"

超大规模的群体性贫困，曾是中国实现人权的最大障碍。改革开放前，近 8 亿人深陷贫困，连温饱都难以解决。

直到 2012 年，中国仍有 9899 万贫困人口。中国举全国之力推进"精准扶贫"，让贫困人口吃穿不愁的同时，义务教育、基本医疗、住房安全等基本人权得到保障。

2020 年底，在经过 30 多年人类历史上规模最大、力度最

---

[1] 国务院新闻办公室：《中国的全面小康》白皮书，2021 年 9 月

强的反贫困斗争后，中国的 7.7 亿农村贫困人口脱贫 [1]，提前 10 年实现联合国 2030 年可持续发展议程的减贫目标，成为世界上减贫人口最多的国家，对全球减贫贡献率超过 70%。

从被当作"会说话的工具"到成为"有尊严的人"，今年 80 岁的西藏自治区山南市克松社区居民洛桑卓玛生活今非昔比：1959 年废除农奴制前，她常年在奴隶主庄园劳作，没有任何收入，不被当人看；现在的她和所有中国人一道迈入全面小康生活，正安享晚年的她感慨万千："过得好、活得幸福，人才有尊严。"

1.2 协调推进"整体人权"

人的各项权利相互联系，相互促进。中国通过保障人的生存权、发展权，促进经济社会文化权利和公民权利、政治权利全面协调发展，整体推进人权事业。

坚持人民至上、生命至上，保障人民生命权、健康权，是中国始终如一的价值遵循。2020 年新冠肺炎疫情暴发以来，中国不放弃救治每一个感染者，从出生仅 30 多个小时的婴儿到 100 多岁的老人，每一个生命都得到全力护佑。面对不断变异的病毒，中国从自身国情出发，科学防控疫情，因时因势不断

---

[1] 国务院新闻办公室：《人类减贫的中国实践》白皮书，2021 年 4 月

调整防控措施，有效统筹疫情防控和经济社会发展工作，最大限度保护人民生命安全和身体健康。

受教育权、工作权、社会保障权等经济社会文化权利的有效保障，让无数中国人的命运得以改变。1975年，18岁的杨德森还在离家200公里的一个小乡村劳动，两年后参加高考，现在已是中国工程院院士、蜚声海内外的水声科学家。杨德森只是千千万万通过教育改变命运的例子之一。

妇女儿童是人权保障的重点群体。新中国第一部法律婚姻法，明确废除包办婚姻，实行婚姻自由、男女平等。中国妇女权利得到极大保障。我国女性平均预期寿命突破80岁，各类高等教育中女生占比均过半，女性就业人数占全社会就业人数超四成。在中国云南丽江华坪女子高级中学，"校长妈妈"张桂梅在10多年间帮助1800多名"大山里的女孩"圆了大学梦。

中国从本国国情实际出发，不断发展全过程人民民主，完善人民当家作主制度体系，建立了人民代表大会制度、中国共产党领导的多党合作和政治协商制度、民族区域自治制度和基层群众自治制度，为人民享有更加广泛、更加充分、更加全面的民主权利奠定了坚实的制度基础。

中国现有49.2万个村民委员会、11.6万个居民委员会，覆盖了城乡的全体居民。2021年完成的新一轮基层自治组织换届，数亿人投票选举产生了近280万名村（居）委会成员。陕西省榆林市郭家伙场村村委会主任高建忠说，现在群众对民主权利的珍视超乎想象，"不少村民从上百公里外赶回来，认认真真投上庄严一票"。

中国民主选举的有效程序

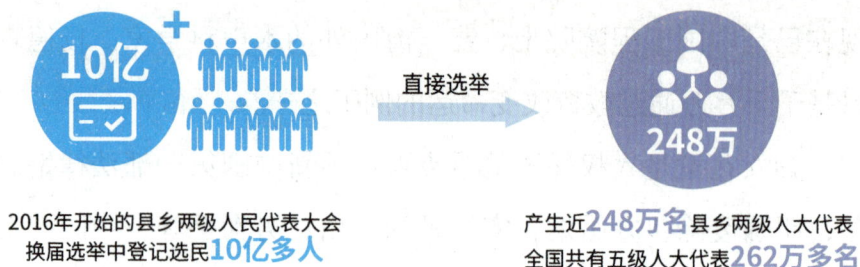

2016年开始的县乡两级人民代表大会
换届选举中登记选民**10亿多人**

直接选举

产生近**248万名**县乡两级人大代表
全国共有五级人大代表**262万多名**

资料来源：《全面建成小康社会：中国人权事业发展的光辉篇章》白皮书

　　中国还不断推进人权法治保障，维护社会公平正义。制定和完善一系列保障人权的法律制度，强化依法行政、加快建设人民满意的法治政府，深化司法体制改革、全面落实司法责任制、坚决纠正和防范冤错案件，增强全社会尊法学法守法用法意识，努力实现尊重和保障人权在立法、执法、司法、守法全链条、全过程、全方位覆盖。2016 年至 2020 年，全国法院通过审判监督程序再审改判刑事案件 8310 起。[1]

―――――――――――――――

[1] 国务院新闻办公室：《国家人权行动计划（2016-2020）》实施成果吹风会，2021 年 5 月 31 日

随着经济社会发展和科技进步，人权的内容不断丰富。2021 年实施的中国第一部民法典明确界定了隐私权，其后又颁布了《中华人民共和国个人信息保护法》，这有效保障了公民私人生活的安宁。此外，中国还颁布《中华人民共和国网络安全法》等法律约束手机应用程序收集消费者个人信息等行为，切实维护公民在网络空间的合法权益。

联合国开发计划署创立的"人类发展指数"综合了预期寿命、教育水平、生活质量等基本指标，是反映人权事业发展的有力印证。得益于"整体人权"的推进，中国人类发展指数大幅提升，从 1990 年的 0.499 上升到 2019 年的 0.761，从低人类发展水平组跨越到高人类发展水平组。

1.3 促进高标准"平等人权"

尽管已全面建成小康社会、成为世界第二大经济体，但发展"不平衡、不充分"仍是中国面临的突出问题。为追求更公平、更全面的人权保障，中国一方面守住民生建设的"底线保障"，同时追求共同富裕的"高线目标"，努力在经济发展中寻找公平与效率的平衡点。

中国建成了世界上规模最大的社会保障体系，这一体系覆盖衣食住行、生老病死，是中国基础性、普惠性、兜底性的民生保障制度设计。"现在看病有医保，60 岁后还有养老金。"

世代生活在黄土高原黄河岸边的农民李东芳说。

中国对人权的保障不是停留在口头上，而是落实到一件件具体的民生实事上，通过脱贫攻坚、危房改造、修路架桥，以及建设饮水工程等，切实提升群众生活水平。以事关生存和健康的环境权为例，中国坚持保护环境基本国策，走可持续发展之路，将环境权写入国家人权行动计划。2012年以来10年间，中国森林面积从31.2亿亩增加到33.54亿亩，人工林面积稳居世界首位。

中国正在进行的共同富裕实践，是更高水平的人权保障追求，将进一步改善人民生活、缩小贫富差距，使全体人民共享发展成果。

1.4 全面参与全球人权治理

中国在发展国内人权事业的同时，积极履行大国责任，大力弘扬和平、发展、公平、正义、民主、自由的全人类共同价值，深度参与联合国人权事务，广泛开展国际人权合作，持续推动全球人权治理，有效促进国际人权事业发展进步。

中国先后批准或加入了30余项国际人权文书，其中包括6项联合国核心人权条约；累计共向166个国家和国际组织提供了援助，派遣60多万名援助人员；多次无条件免除重债穷国和最不发达国家对华到期政府无息贷款债务。在联合国维和行动中，中国是安理会常任理事国第一大出兵国，30 多年来累计派出维和官兵 5 万余人次。共建"一带一路"已成为助力各国发展、深受世界欢迎的新兴国际公共产品，据世界银行研究报告，到 2030 年，将使相关国家 760 万人摆脱极端贫困、3200 万人摆脱中度贫困。新冠肺炎疫情暴发以来，中国努力促进新冠疫苗在全球范围内公平合理分配，成为全球对外提供疫苗数量最多的国家。

"一带一路"、对外国际援助和全球人权贡献

据世界银行研究报告
"一带一路"倡议将使相关国家**760 万人**摆脱极端贫困、**3200 万人**摆脱中度贫困

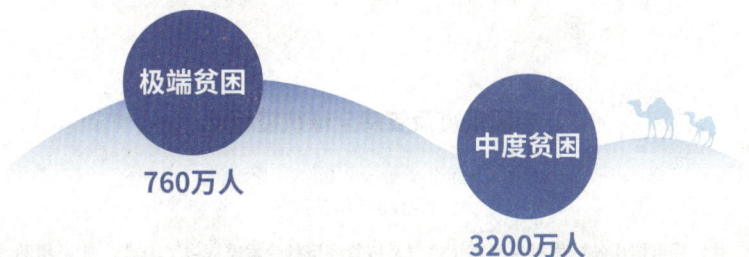

极端贫困

760万人

中度贫困

3200万人

资料来源：《新时代的中国与世界》白皮书

在国际减贫领域，中国大力帮助发展中国家寻找摆脱贫困、实现发展之路，其中菌草技术的推广是"南南合作"的成功范例。20 多年前，中国"以草代木"菌草技术援助项目在巴布亚新几

内亚落地。这一技术如今已推广至全球 100 多个国家。在卢旺达首都基加利，埃马纽埃尔·阿希马纳学到菌草技术后开了一家食用菌培育作坊，收入丰厚。

与此同时，中国积极分享自身减贫经验。中国贵州省惠水县不少农民通过种植佛手瓜实现脱贫。2020 年 9 月，惠水县通过网络直播，向拉美 16 个国家分享经验，70 多个政党和政党组织的 200 多名领导人线上观看讨论。

中国提出的"构建人类命运共同体"理念，多次被写入联合国大会决议、安理会决议、人权理事会决议。中国提出的"发展促进人权"等主张被引入国际人权体系。中国还推动了一系列重要人权文件的制定工作，如《残疾人权利公约》等，持续向国际人权事业贡献中国智慧和中国方案。

中国抗疫及支持全球抗疫行动

截至2021年6月

共为受疫情影响的发展中国家抗疫以及恢复经济社会发展提供了**20亿美元**援助

向**150多个**国家和**13个**国际组织提供了抗疫物资援助

为全球供应了**2900多亿**只口罩
35亿多件防护服
46亿多份检测试剂盒

向**100多个**国家和国际组织
提供**5.2亿**多剂疫苗

资料来源：《中国共产党的历史使命与行动价值》

第二章

人民幸福生活是最大的人权
——当代中国人权观的理论内涵

"人民幸福生活是最大的人权"，是当代中国人权观的高度凝练和概括。以人民为中心的人权理念，明确了中国人权事业发展的价值追求，表明了人民性是中国人权发展道路最显著的特征。

这一理念包含四个维度：在人权主体上，明确人民是人权事业的参与者、促进者，也是最终受益者，人权不是一部分人或少数人享有的特权，而是广大人民群众享有的普惠性人权；在人权内涵上，坚持按人民需求确定人权事业发展方向和重点，将人权从生存权、发展权扩展到其他更多方面，人民对美好生活的向往就是人权事业的奋斗目标；在人权保障上，实行全过程人民民主，充分发挥人民群众的积极性、主动性、创造性，依靠人民推动人权事业的进步和发展；在价值追求上，坚持以人的全面发展为人权最高目标，坚持人民幸福生活是最大的人权，始终维护人民的利益，不断增强人民的获得感、幸福感、安全感。

2.1 当代中国人权观的核心理念、民主要义、民生追求

核心理念——坚持以人民为中心。中国人权事业以保障人民根本利益为出发点和落脚点，坚持为了人民、依靠人民、造福人民、保护人民。以人民为中心，奉行人民至上，坚持人民主体地位，把人民利益摆在至高无上的位置，是中国发展人权事业的最本质特征。

民主要义——坚持人民当家作主。民主权利是基本人权。人民依照宪法和法律规定，通过人民代表大会制度、中国共产党领导的多党合作和政治协商制度、民族区域自治制度和基层群众自治制度，管理国家和社会事务、管理经济和文化事业，成为国家、社会和自己命运的主人，这是中国式民主的核心要义。

民生追求——坚持以民生为人权发展基础。让人民过上好日子，拥有更好的教育、更稳定的工作、更满意的收入、更可靠的社会保障、更高水平的医疗卫生服务、更舒适的居住条件、更优美的环境、更丰富的文化精神生活，让每个人都能免于恐惧、

不受威胁，让每个人更好地发展自我、幸福生活，这是人人享有更加充分人权的真谛，赋予了人权事业发展全新意蕴。

2.2 当代中国人权观的认识论、实践论、辩证法

从认识的角度，坚持人权是历史的、具体的、现实的。人权是在一定经济社会历史条件下的产物，随着历史条件变化而发展，人权保障内容和保障水平也因此不断丰富和提升。人权保障没有最好，只有更好。世界上没有固定的人权保障模式，各国国情不同，历史文化、社会制度、经济社会发展水平存在差异，只能从本国实际和人民需求出发，探索适合自己的人权发展道路。

从实践的角度，坚持以发展促人权。生存是享有一切人权的基础，必须通过发展保障生存，并为其他各项权利的实现创造基础条件。贫困是实现人权的最大障碍，必须通过促进经济发展和社会进步摆脱贫困，并逐步实现共同富裕和全面发展，这是人权保障的中国路径，也是中国人权事业的"发展密码"。

从辩证的角度，坚持个人人权和集体人权有机统一。没有离开个性的共性，也没有离开共性的个性。没有个人的发展就没有集体的发展，离开集体的个人就不能获得全面的发展。必须将个人人权和集体人权统一起来、相互促进，才能实现最大化的人权。

2.3 当代中国人权观的目标定位、法治路径、评价标准

目标定位——促进人的自由全面发展。实现人人享有人权，是人类社会的共同追求。所有人都享有人权，且享有充分的、全面的、高水平的人权，最终实现人的自由全面发展，让每个人都能有尊严地发展自我和奉献社会。

法治路径——维护社会公平正义。公平正义是人类社会发展的永恒主题。通过完善中国特色社会主义制度体系，坚定不移推进全面依法治国，把尊重和保障人权贯穿立法、执法、司法、守法各个环节，以保障权利公平、机会公平和规则公平。

评价标准——人民的获得感、幸福感、安全感。人权不是装饰品，也不是用来做摆设的。人民是历史的创造者，是人权事业的建设者和根本依靠力量。人权状况好不好，应由本国人民来评判，人民的利益是否得到维护，人民的获得感、幸福感、安全感是否得到增强，是评价一国人权状况的最重要标准。

2.4 当代中国人权观的世界情怀

随着经济全球化发展，气候变化、跨国传染性疾病等国际危机不断出现，过时的冷战思维、将本国利益凌驾于他国甚至国际社会的利益之上并且动辄对别国指手画脚的霸权主义做法已经不合时宜。国际关系民主化、国际社会相互依赖甚至依存

关系的增强是客观趋势。[1] 中华民族历来讲求"天下一家"，主张民胞物与、协和万邦、天下大同。当代中国人权观传承中华优秀传统文化基因，主张"大道之行，天下为公"，不仅保证本国人民人权，还"传承仁爱、立己达人"。中国人民愿同世界人民一道，秉持和平、发展、公平、正义、民主、自由的全人类共同价值，维护人的尊严和权利。中国坚持在人权发展道路上，以文明交流超越文明隔阂，以文明互鉴超越文明冲突，以文明共存超越文明优越。中国主张基于平等和互相尊重开展对话和合作，以合作促发展，以发展促人权，推动世界人权事业健康发展。中国坚定不移维护以联合国为核心的国际体系和以国际法为基础的国际秩序，在多边主义框架下大力开展南南合作，推动形成更加公平、公正、合理、包容的全球人权治理。中国关于构建人类命运共同体的理念被写入联合国多个文件，共建"一带一路"，共建人类卫生健康共同体、人与自然生命共同体等主张，以及全球发展倡议、全球安全倡议等倡议，为世界人权事业发展做出贡献，极大地丰富发展了人类人权文明样态。

---

[1] 柳华文，《读懂中国共产党的人权观》，环球时报，2022 年 7 月 29 日

"一带一路"、对外国际援助和全球人权贡献

中国开展对外援助**60多年**来
共向**166个**国家和国际组织提供近**4000亿元**人民币援助

派遣**60多万**名援助人员

700多人为他国发展献出了宝贵生命

资料来源：《新时代的中国与世界》白皮书

第三章

探索尊重和保障人权新境界

——当代中国人权观的借鉴意义

中国在推进人权事业发展实践中，坚持把马克思主义人权观同本国具体实际相结合、同中华优秀传统文化相结合，总结中国共产党团结带领人民尊重和保障人权的成功经验，借鉴人类优秀文明成果，走出了一条顺应时代潮流、适合本国国情的人权发展道路。

作为世界上最大的发展中国家和一个有着深厚文明积淀的东方大国，中国在尊重和保障人权方面的新理念、新举措、新实践，不但为世界人权事业和人类文明画卷增添了新的色彩，也为各国特别是广大发展中国家提供了有益借鉴。中国坚持以生存权、发展权为首要的基本人权，解决了超大规模人口的温饱问题，全面建成小康社会，实现了从大幅落后于时代到大踏步赶上时代的跨越。占世界人口 80% 以上的广大发展中国家也面临着类似课题。正是在这个意义上，中国的探索和经验具有重要参考价值。

美国学者菲利普·李·拉尔夫在《世界文明史》前言写道："迄今人类的进步大多产生于智力的进步和对人权的尊重，其中含有未来更加美好这一主要希望。"中国愿与各国分享经验、共同探索，为推动人类人权文明进步、建设更美好的世界贡献中国智慧和中国方案。

——坚强领导。外国观察者点评中国过去几十年在各领域取得的惊人发展成就时，常常聚焦于中国规模化治理经验的一个鲜明特点——领导力，其中包括"一张蓝图绘到底"的顶层设计、领导者以"钉钉子精神"抓落实，以及强大的社会动员力。

对广大发展中国家来说，从实现国家独立、民族解放到致力发展经济、改善民生，拥有一个坚强有力的领导者至关重要。在中国，"领导者"就是中国共产党。中国共产党以"为中国人民谋幸福、为中华民族谋复兴"为初心使命，将"一盘散沙"的中国人民团结组织起来，完成了现代国家的建构与重塑，使人民成为国家、社会和自己命运的主人，通过提升国家能力、完善国家治理，推动实现超大人口规模的现代化转型，并在这一转型过程中为人民提供权益福祉、创造美好生活。在中国的脱贫攻坚战中，习近平主席亲自谋划、靠前指挥，走遍全国 14 个集中连片特困地区，25.5 万个驻村工作队、300 多万名第一书记和驻村干部，同近 200 万名乡镇干部和数百万村干部奋战在减贫一线，中国仅用了 8 年时间就实现了近 1 亿农村贫困人口的脱贫，创造了世界人权史上的奇迹。

中国共产党的坚强领导，使中国人权事业具有了清晰的战略指向，形成了高效的聚合能力，不断激发了人民群众的积极性、主动性、创造性。中国将抽象的人权概念具体化为生存权、发展权、生命权、健康权等一系列人民群众实实在在享有的权益，使人权更加具体可感，促进了人权事业的发展。

——**立足实际**。对大量生活在动荡地区的儿童来说，人权首先意味着保障生命安全，并离开难民营、回到安宁的家园和课堂；对欠发达国家妇女来说，人权可能意味着在家门口拥有一口水井、喝上干净充足的饮用水；对深受能源危机影响的家庭来说，人权可能意味着获得负担得起的现代能源，可以在明亮的灯光中与家人共进晚餐；对许多美国少数族裔来说，人权可能首先意味着在生活、工作等领域免于遭受系统性歧视，得到公平的个人和家庭发展机会。

世界上没有两片完全相同的树叶，人权事业发展也不能套用"一个模子"。中国的实践表明，从自身实际出发，走符合本国国情的人权发展道路，才能行得通、走得顺、为人民所满意。各国的情况千差万别，理应根据自身国情，选择适合自己的人权发展道路。强加的"人权道路"往往行不通，简单的人权"拿来主义"通常会"水土不服"。

——发展驱动。人权保障离不开一定的物质基础。发展是实现人民幸福的途径，也是推动人权事业进步的动力。中国政府始终把发展作为优先事项，通过做大经济"蛋糕"，夯实人权保障的物质基础。同时，顺应人民对高品质美好生活的期待，通过更高质量、更有效率、更加公平、更可持续、更为安全的发展，不断满足人民日益增长的多方面权利需求，促进各项人权的全面发展。

在历史性地解决了绝对贫困这一人权的最大障碍后，中国又着眼于共同富裕，努力使发展成果更公平地惠及全体人民，通过发展力求使每一个个体的获得感、幸福感、安全感更加充实、更有保障、更可持续。

当今世界，百年未有之大变局加速演进，大国博弈加剧，地区冲突频仍，世纪疫情持续蔓延，世界人权事业遭受严峻挑战。在这一背景下，发展的意义愈发凸显。中国提出全球发展倡议，就是要推动落实联合国2030年可持续发展议程，实现更加强劲、绿色、健康的全球发展，在发展中更好地保障和增进人权。

——法治保障。法治是人类政治文明的重要成果，是现代国家治理的基本方式，也是保障人权的有效途径。中国在推动人权事业发展中，十分注重法治保障。《中华人民共和国宪法》为保障人权提供了根本依据和根本规范，不仅确立了"国家尊重和保障人权"原则，还全面系统地规定了全体人民享有广泛的人身人格权利、财产权利、政治权利和经济、社会、文化权利。

中国实施全面依法治国战略，以中国特色社会主义法治体系建设引领依法治国、依法执政、依法行政共同推进，法治国家、法治政府、法治社会一体建设，为维护公民各项权益提供坚强保障。

——互鉴包容。近代人权概念、思想、实践诞生于欧洲启蒙运动。数百年来，尊重和保障人权既是现代文明的基本精神，也是人类文明进步的重要标志。就像《世界人权宣言》被译成数百种不同语言在全球广泛传播，发展人权这项全人类的共同事业也在世界各地形成了丰富多样的发展路径。

由于历史文化、社会制度、经济社会发展水平不同，各国人民对人权的认识理解和发展路径的选择也不尽相同。中国尊重人权实践的多样性，认为在人权问题上不存在十全十美的"理想国"，反对在人权问题上搞"双重标准"，反对将人权问题政治化、工具化、武器化，反对以人权为借口干涉别国内政。中国主张加强不同文明交流互鉴，解决全球人权"治理赤字"，推动形成更加公平、公正、合理、包容的全球人权治理，共同构建人类命运共同体。

结　语

　　人权保障没有最好，只有更好。

　　经过长期艰苦奋斗，中国成功走出了一条顺应时代潮流、适合本国国情的人权发展道路。作为世界最大发展中国家，中国仍将长期处于社会主义初级阶段，人权事业还有很大发展空间。在实现第一个百年奋斗目标后，中国已开启全面建设社会主义现代化国家新征程。在新的发展起点上，中国顺应人民对美好生活的向往，更加重视尊重和保障人权，统筹推进经济建设、政治建设、文化建设、社会建设和生态文明建设，不断满足人民日益增长的多方面权利需求，全方位提升各项人权保障水平。

　　放眼当今世界，贫困、战乱、环境等问题对人权保护构成严重威胁，全球人权"治理赤字"十分突出。针对这些威胁，世界各国需要团结，而不是对抗；需要合作，而不是脱钩；需要开放，而不是封锁；需要沟通，而不是制裁。

　　实现人人充分享有人权，是人类社会的共同追求。各国应在平等和尊重的基础上，积极开展人权对话和合作，扩大共识、减少分歧、相互借鉴、共同进步，使全球人权治理更加公平、公正、合理、包容，真正造福各国人民。

For a Life of Contentment

The Rationale for China's Human Rights Development

December 2022

Introduction

It is a great dream of the human society that everyone can enjoy human rights in the full sense of the term.

Given the diversity of civilizations, each country is unique with its own history, culture and institutions, as well as its particular development level and path. But promoting and protecting human rights has been a common pursuit of the entire international community.

The emphasis on human dignity and values and the people-centered philosophy are deeply rooted in traditional Chinese virtues, and have been followed throughout China's human rights progress. More than 2000 years ago, Chinese philosophers proposed that "man of all creatures is one endowed with intelligence" and that "Nothing is more valuable in the universe than human beings". According to Confucianism, the philosophy with the greatest influence on the Chinese people, "a benevolent person loves others," treats people sincerely and kindly, and upholds human dignity with compassion. When "the widowed, lonely, disabled and ill can all be cared for," and people deal with interpersonal and social relations harmoniously and genially, the society will embrace good fortune and people will be united for a common cause.

The Universal Declaration of Human Rights is the crystallization of such lofty aspirations of mankind. All human beings, so reads the first article, are "endowed with reason and conscience." Conscience is the embodiment of the concept of benevolence cherished by Chinese Confucianism. The phrase contains a strong "Chinese conscience," and is saturated with oriental wisdom between the lines.

In the practice of promoting human rights progress, China has followed a path of human rights development that conforms to the trend of the times and suits its national conditions, by combining the Marxist outlook on human rights with the country's actual conditions and the fine traditional Chinese culture, while drawing on outstanding achievements of other civilizations.

A staunch defender of human rights, the Communist Party of China (CPC) has since its founding united and led the Chinese people of all ethnic groups in making unremitting efforts to fight for, respect, protect and develop human rights. It is under the leadership of the Party that China's human rights cause has achieved all-round development, made historic achievements, and created a miracle of rapid economic development and long-term social stability that has rarely been seen in world history.

China's outlook on human rights has been continuously enriched and improved in practice, with its own cognitive perspective and ideological connotation based on the actual conditions of the country. China is committed to protecting and promoting human rights in development, and follows the "development-based approach to human rights." Hunger that once threatened the lives of hundreds of millions of people has made China keenly aware that poverty is the biggest obstacle to the realization of human rights, and that the rights to subsistence and development are the primary basic human rights. Colonial aggression against China following the Opium War has led the nation to fully understand that it is impossible to talk about human rights without sovereignty, and difficult to safeguard certain individuals' human rights without collective rights?

Human rights have historical, specific and practical contexts, and there are no fixed standards or identical models for its development and protection. The development path of human rights in each country should be respected, and the human rights conditions of that country should be judged by its own people. Based on the human rights philosophy that centers on the people, China has proposed that "living a life of contentment is the ultimate human right."

As pointed out in the report to 20th CPC National Congress: This country is its people; the people are the country. As the Communist Party of China has led the people in fighting to establish and develop the People's Republic, it has really been fighting for their support. Bringing benefit to the people is the fundamental principle of governance. Working for the people's wellbeing is an essential part of the Party's commitment to serving the public good and exercising governance for the people. We must ensure and improve the people's wellbeing in the course of pursuing development and encourage everyone to work hard together to meet the people's aspirations for a better life.

We must strive to realize, safeguard, and advance the fundamental interests of all our people. To this end, we must do everything within our capacity to resolve the most practical problems that are of the greatest and most direct concern to the people. We will stay engaged with our people and their communities, adopt more measures that deliver real benefits to the people and win their approval, and work hard to resolve the pressing difficulties and problems that concern them most. We will improve the basic public services system by raising public service standards and making public services more balanced and accessible, so as to achieve solid progress in promoting common prosperity.

The journey of China's human rights development is both rich and colorful, systematic and pragmatic. The country has formed a contemporary Chinese outlook on human rights with "people" as the center, "development" as the driving force and "a life of contentment" as the goal through continuous progress, and has enriched the global human rights cause.

Chapter 1

The Basics: Rights to Subsistence, Development, Dignity and Happiness

---

The Communist Party of China and the Chinese government have included respecting and protecting human rights as a key part of national governance, and thanks to this, China's human rights cause has delivered historic achievement.

"In the past, many people lived their whole lives without a single good day." Chu Chengming, an elderly farmer living in the Dabie Mountains, said emotionally as he browsed through his family tree.

According to the genealogical records, his grandfather raised 10 children, five of whom died young. His father was born shortly after Aisin-Gioro Puyi, the last emperor of the Qing Dynasty (1644-1911), ascended the throne, and died in the War of Resistance Against Japanese Aggression in 1944 at the age of just 36. His mother died at 47.

The record of this ordinary family is the epitome of modern China's reality — people suffering from war, poverty and diseases, with no protection whatsoever for human rights. When the People's Republic of China was founded in 1949, the average life expectancy in the country was less than 35 years old.

In today's China, the lack of food, clothing and medical services is long gone. Since the beginning of the reform and opening up drive more than 40 years ago, the per capita disposable income in China has increased by more than 180 times. Some 770 million rural Chinese have been lifted out of poverty and live a moderately prosperous life. The average life expectancy has risen to 78.2 years.[1]

Under the leadership of the CPC, the fate of countless people has been changed. A new chapter has been written in the history of China's human rights by the earth-shaking changes in the Chinese society, and the country has seen achievement in the human rights cause on all fronts. China deems the rights to subsistence and development as the primary basic human rights. The CPC is an active promoter and staunch defender of the human rights cause, and has always included respecting and protecting human rights as a key part of national governance. The country has formulated and implemented national human rights action plans and other special plans, to promote human rights development through protection, and to advance the human rights cause through development. It made step-by-step achievements of raising the living standards of its people from poverty to bare subsistence, from moderate prosperity in general to moderate prosperity in all aspects. The country has embarked on a journey of pursuing a higher goal of common prosperity, and is committed to providing a happy and dignified life for some one fifth of the world's population.

1.1 Removing the "biggest obstacle to human rights" for 1.4 billion people

Mass poverty on an enormous scale was once the biggest obstacle in China's

---

[1] State Council Information Office: White paper titled "China's Epic Journey from Poverty to Prosperity," September 2021.

human rights cause. Before the launch of reform and opening up, nearly 800 million people were impoverished, unable to meet their basic living needs.

By 2012, there were still 98.99 million people living in poverty in China. China made a nationwide effort to promote "targeted poverty alleviation," so that the remaining poor population could access sufficient food and clothing, while their other basic human rights such as compulsory education, basic medical care and housing security, were also promoted and protected.

By the end of 2020, after more than 30 years of fighting poverty, the largest and strongest such campaign in human history, China had lifted over 770 million rural poor out of poverty1. The country met the poverty eradication target of the 2030 Agenda for Sustainable Development 10 years ahead of schedule. With the highest number of people lifted out of poverty, China has contributed to over 70 percent of global poverty reduction.

From being regarded as "a talking tool" to becoming "a person with dignity," 80-year-old Losang Droma from the Khesum Community in the city of Shannan, Tibet Autonomous Region, has witnessed profound life changes: Before the abolition of serfdom in 1959, she worked in the slave owner's manor all year round without any income, and she was not treated as a person of dignity. Now, together with all Chinese people, she is living a moderately prosperous life. While enjoying her retirement, she said, "only those who live well and happily can have dignity."

1.2 Promoting "holistic human rights" in a coordinated way

Every kind of human rights is interrelated and mutually reinforcing. By safeguarding people's rights to subsistence and development and promoting the comprehensive and coordinated development of economic, social and cultural rights as well as the civil and political rights of its citizens, China has advanced the cause of human rights with a holistic approach.

It is China's consistent value to put the people and their lives first and to protect people's right to life and health. Since the outbreak of COVID-19 in 2020, China has spared no effort to save every infected patient. From a 30-hour-old baby to the elderly of over 100 years old, every life has been protected with the utmost effort. In the face of the constantly mutating virus, China has carried out scientific prevention and control of the epidemic based on its own national conditions, constantly adjusted prevention and control measures in response to the changing situation, effectively coordinated epidemic prevention and control with economic and social development, and protected people's lives and health to the greatest extent.

The effective protection of economic, social and cultural rights such as the right to education, work and social security has changed the fortunes of countless Chinese people. In 1975, Yang Desen, then aged 18, was working in a small village 200 kilometers from his home. Two years later, he took the college entrance examination and is now a member of the Chinese Academy of Engineering and a well-known underwater acoustic scientist. Yang Desen is just one of millions of examples of people changing their lives through education.

Women and children are key groups in the protection of human rights. The Marriage Law, the first piece of legislation promulgated by the People's Republic of China, explicitly abolished arranged marriage and enshrined freedom of marriage and gender equality. Women's rights are strictly protected in China. The average life expectancy of Chinese women currently exceeds 80 years, while women account for more than half of higher education students and take up over 40 percent of the jobs in the country. In the city of Lijiang in Yunnan Province, Zhang Guimei, who runs the Huaping Senior High School for Girls, has helped more than 1,800 rural girls over the past ten years to realize their college dreams.

Based on its own national conditions, China has constantly developed its whole-process people's democracy, and improved

the system of institutions through which the people exercise their role as masters of the country. The country established the system of people's congresses, the system of CPC-led multiparty cooperation and political consultation, the system of regional ethnic autonomy and the system of community-level self-governance, laying a solid institutional foundation for the people to enjoy broader, fuller and more comprehensive democratic rights.

Effective procedures for democratic elections in China

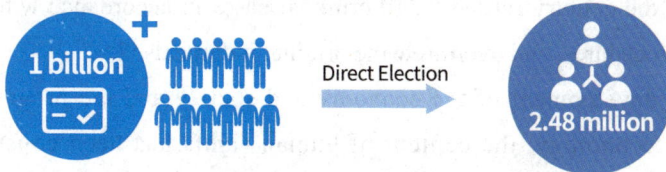

1 billion

Direct Election

2.48 million

More than 1 billion voters were registered in elections for the people's congresses at the county and township levels which started in 2016.

Nearly 2.48 million deputies were elected to people's congresses at the county and township levels.There are more than 2.62 million deputies to the people's congresses at five levels.

Source: Moderate Prosperity in All Respects: Another Milestone Achieved in China's Human Rights (White Paper)

China now has 492,000 villagers' committees and 116,000 residents' committees, covering all residents in both urban and rural areas. In the latest elections for grassroots self-governing organizations completed in 2021, hundreds of millions of people voted and elected nearly 2.8 million members of the committees of local villagers and residents. Gao Jianzhong, head of the villager's committee of Guojiahuochang Village in Yulin city, Shaanxi Province, said the extent of how much people now cherish democratic rights was beyond imagination. "Many villagers came back from hundreds of kilometers away to cast their votes."

China has also promoted legal protection for human rights and safeguarded social equity and justice. It has formulated and improved a series of legal systems to protect human rights, strengthened law-based governance, sped up the building of a law-based government that the people are satisfied with, deepened reform of the judicial system, fully implemented the judicial responsibility system, resolutely redressed and prevented wrongful convictions and false charges, enhanced people's awareness of the need to respect, study and abide by the law and their ability to apply the law, and striven to respect and protect human rights in the whole process of legislation, law enforcement, administration of justice and observance of the law. From 2016 to 2020, courts across the country retried 8,310 criminal cases in accordance with trial supervision procedures, and overthrew the original judgments.[1]

With the development of the economy and society and the progress of science and technology, the content of human rights has been constantly enriched. The right to privacy was clearly defined in China's first Civil Code, which took effect in 2021. China also promulgated the Law on Protection of Personal Information, which effectively guarantees citizens' privacy. In addition, China has promulgated the Cybersecurity Law and other laws to restrict the collection of consumers' personal information by mobile apps, effectively safeguarding citizens' legitimate rights and interests in cyberspace.

The Human Development Index (HDI), created by the United Nations Development Programme by integrating basic indicators such as life expectancy, education level and quality of life, is a credible proof of human rights progress. Thanks to the improvement of "holistic human rights," China's HDI rose from 0.499 in 1990 to 0.761 in 2019, ascending from the ranks of countries with low HDI scores to the ranks of those with high HDI scores.

[1] State Council Information Office: Briefing on the Implementation Results of the National Human Rights Action Plan of China (2016-2020), May 31, 2021

1.3 Promoting high standards of "equal human rights"

Although China has finished building a moderately prosperous society in all respects and become the world's second-largest economy, "unbalanced and inadequate" development is still a salient challenge the country faces. In the pursuit of fairer and more comprehensive protection of human rights, China upholds the "bottom-line guarantee" of ensuring basic living standards, and at the same time pursues the "high-line goal" of common prosperity, striving to strike a balance between fairness and efficiency in economic development.

China has built the world's largest social security network, which covers nearly all aspects of people's daily lives. It is a system for ensuring people's well-being that can provide inclusive public services, meet essential needs and ensure basic living standards. "We've got medical insurance, and we have pension after turning 60," said Li Dongfang, a farmer whose family has lived on the banks of the Yellow River on the Loess Plateau for generations.

China's protection of human rights is not just paying lip service, but implemented through concrete actions. By eliminating extreme poverty, renovating dilapidated houses, constructing roads and bridges, and building drinking water projects, China has effectively improved people's living standards. Take environmental rights, which are crucial to the survival and health of its people, as another example. China upholds the basic national policy of environmental protection, follows the path of sustainable development, and includes the right to the environment in its national human rights action plan. In the 10 years since 2012, China's forest area has increased from 208 million hectares to 223.6 million hectares, ranking first in the world in planted forest area.

China's ongoing practice of common prosperity is the pursuit of a higher level of human rights protection, which will further improve people's lives, narrow the wealth gap, and enable all people to share the benefits of development.

1.4 Fully participating in global human rights governance

While advancing its human rights cause at home, China also actively fulfills its responsibilities as a big country, by vigorously promoting the common values of peace, development, fairness, justice, democracy and freedom, by engaging deeply in UN human rights affairs, and by extensively carrying out international human rights cooperation, thus continuously promoting global human rights governance and effectively promoting international human rights development and progress.

China has successively ratified or acceded to more than 30 international human rights instruments, including six core UN conventions. It has provided assistance to 166 countries and international organization, and sent over 600,000 people on aid missions. It has also canceled matured government interest-free debts owed by heavily indebted poor countries, and least-developed countries on several occasions. China ranks first among the permanent members of the UN Security Council in terms of the number of peacekeepers dispatched, having sent more than 50,000 personnel on peacekeeping missions over the last three decades. The Belt and Road Initiative has become a new international public good that supports the development   of all countries and is well received by the world. According to a World Bank report, the initiative could contribute to lifting 7.6 million people from extreme poverty and 32 million from moderate poverty. Since the outbreak of COVID-19, China has made great efforts to promote fair and reasonable distribution of COVID-19 vaccines around the world, and has become the country providing the largest number of vaccines to the rest of the world.

In terms of global poverty relief, China has actively assisted developing countries in seeking ways to shake off poverty and achieve development. Among these efforts, the Juncao technology project, which uses grass instead of wood to cultivate edible fungi, is an exemplary model in South-South cooperation.

Over two decades ago, China launched the Juncao assistance project in Papua New Guinea. So far, the technology has taken root in more than 100 countries. In Kigali, capital of Rwanda, Emmanuel Ahimana learned to apply Juncao technology to grow mushrooms and has now been handsomely rewarded.

The Belt and Road Initiative, China's foreign aid, and its contributions to global human rights development

According to a World Bank report,
the Belt and Road Initiative could contribute to lifting **7.6 million** people from extreme poverty and **32 million** from moderate poverty.

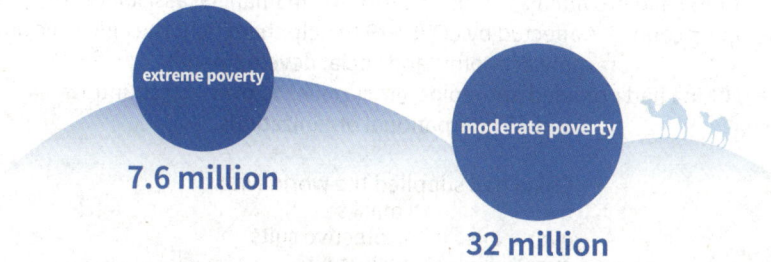

extreme poverty

7.6 million

moderate poverty

32 million

Source: China and the World in the New Era (White Paper)

In the meantime, China also actively shares its experience in poverty alleviation with the world. In September 2020, Huishui County, southwest China's Guizhou Province, hosted a livestream discussion with over 200 politicians from 16 Latin American countries, and shared its experience of how local farmers had shaken off poverty by growing chayote.

The vision of "a community of shared future for mankind" put forward by China has been written into the resolutions of the UN General Assembly, the UN Security Council and the UN Human Rights Council on multiple occasions. A series of propositions put forth by China, including the concept of "promoting human rights through development," have been introduced into the sphere of international human rights. China also facilitated the formulation of a number of important documents on human rights, such as the Convention on the Rights of Persons with Disabilities (CRPD). The country has continuously offered the world Chinese wisdom and solutions to promote the global cause of human rights.

China's anti-epidemic efforts and its support for global COVID-19 response

As of June 2021
China had provided 2 billion U.S. dollars in financial assistance to developing countries affected by COVID-19 to help them fight the epidemic and resume economic and social development.
China had provided anti-epidemic supplies to over 150 countries and 13 international organizations.

China had supplied the world with
over 290 billion masks
over 3.5 billion protective suits
over 4.6 billion testing kits

and provided over 520 million doses of COVDI-19 vaccines to over 100 countries and international organizations

Source: The CPC: Its Mission and Contributions

Chapter 2

The Rationale: Living a Life of Contentment is the Ultimate Human Right

---

"Living a life of contentment is the ultimate human right."

— This is the essence of China's rationale for human rights development. The people-centered concept of human rights defines the value China pursues in its human rights cause, and shows that putting emphasis on the people is the distinguishing feature of the Chinese path of human rights protection.

This concept includes four dimensions. In terms of the subject of human rights, it makes clear that the people are participants, promoters and ultimate beneficiaries of the cause of human rights. Human rights are not privileges enjoyed by a certain group or by just a few people, but inclusive rights enjoyed by the broad masses of the people. In terms of the connotation of human rights, the direction and focus of human rights development are set in line with the needs of the people. Human rights are expanded from the rights to subsistence and development to other aspects, and the people's aspiration for a better life is the goal of the human rights cause. In terms of human rights protection, whole-process people's democracy is implemented, which gives full play to the enthusiasm, initiative and creativity of the people, so that the people are relied on to drive the progress and development of human rights. In terms of the pursuit of values, the well-rounded development of the individuals is taken as the supreme goal of human rights and living a life of contentment is regarded as the ultimate human right. The people's interests are constantly safeguarded and their sense of gain, happiness and security continuously enhanced.

2.1 The core philosophy, the principle of democracy, and the focus on people's livelihoods

The core philosophy — to remain committed to being people-centered. China's human rights cause takes safeguarding fundamental interests of the people as its starting point and ultimate goal. It is committed to serving, relying on, benefiting and protecting the people. Putting people first, upholding the principal position of the people, and putting the interests of the people above all else are the fundamental features of China's human rights development.

The principle of democracy — to remain committed to people being masters of their own country. Democratic rights are the basic human rights. In accordance with China's Constitution and laws, the people manage state and social affairs, economic and cultural undertakings and become masters of the country, society and their own destiny through the system of people's congresses, the system of CPC-led multiparty cooperation and political consultation, the system of regional ethnic autonomy and the system of community-level self-governance. This is the core essence of Chinese-style democracy.

The focus on people's livelihoods — to remain committed to people's well-being as the foundation of human rights development. To make sure that people live a good life, and enjoy better education, more stable employment, more satisfactory incomes, more reliable social security, higher-level medical and health services, more comfortable housing, a more beautiful environment and a richer cultural and intellectual life, make everyone free from fear and threat, and let everyone better develop themselves and live a happy life, these are the essence of people fully enjoying more human rights, giving new meaning to progress in human rights.

Composition of deputies to China's National People's Congress

15.7% are workers and farmers

Of the deputies to the 13th National People's Congress

As of April 2021, there were more than 2.62 million deputies to the people's congresses nationwide at all levels in China.

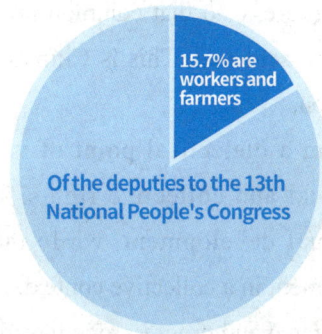

Source: The Communist Party of China and Human Rights Protection — A 100-Year Quest (White Paper)

2.2 The theoretical rationale

From an epistemological point of view, human rights are historical, concrete and realistic. Human rights are the product of certain economic, social and historical conditions, and they develop with the changes of historical conditions. In this sense, the content and level of human rights protection are constantly enriched and improved. There is no end to improving human rights. There is no fixed model of human rights protection in the world. Countries vary in national conditions, histories, cultures, social systems and economic and social development levels. A proper path of human rights development should be explored to suit national conditions and the needs of the people.

From a practical point of view, human rights are promoted through development. Subsistence is the foundation for enjoying all human rights, and development is a must to guarantee subsistence and a foundation for the fulfillment of all other rights. Poverty is the greatest obstacle to human rights, and it must be shaken off through promoting economic development and social progress, so that common prosperity and well-rounded development are gradually achieved. This is China's key approach to advancing human rights protection.

From a dialectical point of view, human rights are the integration of individual and collective rights. There is no collective progress without individual development, while individuals can only enjoy well-rounded development in a collective context. Individual and collective human rights must be integrated and progress side by side, in order to achieve optimal development of human rights.

2.3　The objective, law-based governance, and the evaluation criteria

The objective — promoting the free and well-rounded development of individuals. It is the common pursuit of humanity to realize human rights for all. All people should enjoy full, comprehensive and high-level human rights, so that the free and all-round development of every individual can be ultimately realized, and everyone can fulfill self-development themselves and contribute to the society with dignity.

The roadmap marked by rule of law — upholding social fairness and justice. The principle of equity and justice is the eternal theme of the development of human society. Through improving the socialist institutional frameworks with Chinese characteristics and steadfastly advancing law-based governance, China has integrated the practice of respecting and protecting human rights into the whole process of legislation, law enforcement, administration of justice, and observance of law, to ensure equal rights, equal opportunities and fair rules for all.

The evaluation criteria — people's sense of gain, of happiness, and of security. Human rights are not an ornament to be used for decoration. The people are the creators of history, and the builders and the fundamental force to rely on in the human rights cause. A country's human rights are essentially gauged by its own people. Whether the people's interests are safeguarded and whether their sense of gain, happiness and security is enhanced are important criteria for evaluating a country's human rights situation.

2.4 Global vision

In the wake of economic globalization and international challenges such as climate change and transnational infectious diseases, the Cold War mentality as well as the hegemonic practices of putting one's own country's interests above the interests of others and even the international community at large, and pointing fingers at other countries are not welcome. The democratization of international relations and the reinforcement of interdependence of the international community is an objective trend.[1]

The Chinese nation has always held these beliefs dear: "All people under the heaven are of one family" "All the people are my brothers and I share the

---

[1] Liu Huawen, "Understanding the Communist Party of China's view of human rights," the Global Times, July 29, 2022

life of all creatures" and "All nations should live in harmony." China's outlook on human rights has deep cultural roots, advocating that "a just cause should be pursued for the common good," which not only guarantees the human rights of the Chinese people, but also strives to pass down the spirit of benevolence and pursue one's own development as well as development for all. The Chinese people are ready to work with people all over the world to uphold the common values of peace, development, fairness, justice, democracy and freedom for all mankind, and to safeguard human dignity and rights.

On the path of human rights development, China is committed to replacing estrangement between civilizations with exchanges, clashes with mutual learning, and superiority with co-existence. China advocates dialogue and cooperation based on equality and mutual respect, and seeks to promote progress through cooperation and to ensure human rights with benefits deriving from development, so as to promote the healthy development of the global human rights cause.

China firmly upholds the international system with the United Nations (UN) at its core and the international order based on international law, vigorously conducts South-South cooperation under the framework of multilateralism, and work toward the formation of a fairer, more equitable, reasonable and inclusive global human rights governance system. The notion of building a human community with a shared future has been written into many UN documents. The ideas including jointly building the Belt and Road and jointly building a global community of health for all as well as a community of life for man and Nature, and the initiatives including the Global Development Initiative and the Global Security Initiative, have all contributed to the cause of global human rights development, and have greatly enriched and developed the concept of human rights.

The Belt and Road Initiative, China's foreign aid, and its contributions to global human rights development

Over the past more than **60 years** since China began to provide foreign assistance, the country has provided nearly **400 billion** yuan in development aid to **166** countries and international organizations

China has dispatched over **600,000** people on aid missions

More than **700** aid workers sacrificed their lives for the development of other countries

Source: China and the World in the New Era (White Paper)

Chapter 3

The Implications: Exploring New Dimensions in Respecting and Protecting Human Rights

China is the largest developing country in the world and a vast country with an ancient history. Its novel ideas, measures and practices in terms of how to respect and protect human rights are a refreshing addition to the global human rights cause and to the diversity of civilizations. They may also offer inspiration for the rest of the world, especially for developing countries. By upholding the idea that the rights to subsistence and development should be taken as primary basic human rights, China has met the basic living needs for an extra-large population and finished building a moderately prosperous society in all respects. With a combined population of more than 80 percent of the world's total, developing countries are faced with similar tasks. In this sense, China's explorations and experiences are of great value for their reference.

American scholar Philip Lee Ralph wrote in the preface of *World Civilizations* that "most of human progress thus far has resulted from the growth of intelligence and respect for the rights of man, and that therein lies the chief hope for a better world in the future". China is ready to share its experiences with the rest of the world, engage in joint explorations, and contribute Chinese wisdom and proposals to the global initiatives to advance human rights and build a better world.

— **Determined Leadership.** When commenting on the incredible achievements that China has made in various fields over the past few decades, foreign observers are often impressed by its leadership, which is a distinctive feature of the country's experience in governance. This is best manifested in the top-level design that allows for blueprints to be translated into reality, the perseverance to hammer away until a job is done, and strong mobilization capabilities.

For developing countries, a strong leadership is of vital importance to their many endeavors ranging from national independence and liberation to economic growth and improvement of people's livelihood.

Taking as its original aspiration and mission the pursuit of happiness for the Chinese people and rejuvenation for the Chinese nation, the CPC has successfully united and organized the Chinese people in building China into a modern country, and made the people masters of the country, of the society and of their very own fate. During the past decades, the Party has been working hard to advance the modernization of the country, while ensuring people's well-being and raising their living standards. As China's fight against poverty entered its decisive stage, President Xi Jinping personally planned and commanded the battle at the forefront, having visited 14 contiguous areas of dire poverty. Throughout the country, 255,000 resident working teams and more than 3 million first Party secretaries and officials stationed in poor villages fought poverty on the front line alongside nearly 2 million township officials and millions more cadres dispatched to villages. At a result, it only took China eight years to lift 100 million rural dwellers out of poverty, creating a miracle in the history of human rights.

The strong leadership of the CPC has provided clear strategic guidance for China's human rights cause, fostered efficient synergy capabilities, and unleashed the enthusiasm, initiative, and creativity of the people in a continuous manner. China has turned the abstract concept of human rights into a set of tangible rights and interests that the people could enjoy on the ground, such as the rights to subsistence, development, life and health. This has made human rights more concrete and appreciable, marking a major advancement of the human rights cause.

— **Down-to-Earth Approach.** For children living in war-torn regions, human rights are first and foremost defined as personal safety and being able to leave the refugee camps and return to their peaceful homes and classrooms. For women in underdeveloped countries, human rights might mean a water well near their doorsteps and sufficient, clean drinking water. For families mired in energy crises, human rights may refer to access to affordable modern energy that would allow them to have dinner in bright lamplight. For many racial minorities in the United States, human rights might come first and foremost as being free from systemic discrimination in life and at work and receiving equitable opportunities for personal and family development.

There are no two identical leaves in the world. Likewise, there is no single fixed model for the development of the human rights cause. China's experience suggests that a path that is based on the realities of the country itself and befits its own conditions is the only one that can work well, and win the support of its people. Countries vary significantly in national conditions, thus they ought to choose paths that conform to their circumstances and befit themselves. Paths imposed by others usually lead to nowhere, whereas blind imitation often backfires.

— **Development-Oriented.** Human rights protection would not be possible without certain material prerequisites. Development is the pathway to people's well-being, and the driver for the advancement of the human rights cause. The Chinese government has always prioritized development, and kept expanding the economic pie to ensure a solid material foundation for human rights protection. To meet people's aspirations for a quality life, the government has pursued a development path that is of higher-quality, more efficient, equitable, sustainable and secure to keep up with the people's ever-growing needs for multifaceted rights, and facilitate all-round progress of each human right.

After securing the historic success of eradicating absolute poverty, which is considered the biggest obstacle to human rights, China has set its eyes on the undertaking of common prosperity, working to distribute the benefits of development among the people in a fairer way and provide them with a more robust, solid, and sustainable sense of gain, happiness, and security.

The world today is undergoing profound changes unseen in a century. The global human rights cause faces grave challenges. Against such a backdrop, development carries much more salient relevance. The Global Development Initiative that China has proposed aims to facilitate the implementation of the UN 2030 Agenda for Sustainable Development, so as to achieve more robust, greener and more balanced global development, and, in turn, better protect and enhance human rights.

— **Legal Guidance.** Rule of law is an important political achievement of mankind, a basic way of modern governance, and an effective instrument to protect human rights. When advancing its human rights cause, China attaches great importance to strengthening of legal protection. China's Constitution serves as a fundamental document for safeguarding human rights, and sets basic terms in this regard. It not only establishes that the state shall respect and protect human rights, but also makes comprehensive and systematic stipulations to ensure that all citizens enjoy personal rights, the right to dignity, property rights, political rights, and economic, social and cultural rights. China has implemented a strategy to comprehensively advance the rule of law. It strives to build a system of socialist rule of law with Chinese characteristics to pursue coordinated progress in law-based governance, law-based exercise of state power and law-based government administration, and promote integrated development of the country, the government, and society based on the rule of law, so that the citizens' rights and interests are firmly ensured.

— **Open-Mindedness.** The modern concept, thinking and practices of human rights were born during the Enlightenment in Europe. Hundreds of years on, respecting and protecting human rights have become a fundamental principle of modern civilization and a great hallmark of the advancement of civilization. As the Universal Declaration of Human Rights has been translated into hundreds of languages and spread across the globe, human rights, a common undertaking shared by mankind, have been developed along diverse pathways in the world.

Given the differences in history, culture, social systems, and economic and social development, people from different countries of the world have different understandings of human rights and pursue different paths to seek human rights progress. China respects the diversity in the approaches to human rights development and holds that there is no such thing as a perfect "Utopia" for human rights. It opposes double standards in human rights, rejects attempts to politicize and weaponize human rights, and objects to interventions in others' internal affairs in the name of human rights. China advocates enhanced exchanges and mutual learning between civilizations, addressing the "governance deficit" of human rights, promoting fairer, more equitable, reasonable and inclusive global governance of human rights, and working together to build a human community with a shared future.

Conclusion

The quest to improve human rights never ends.

After decades of strenuous efforts, China has successfully blazed a human rights development path that conforms to the times and befits its own national conditions. As the largest developing country in the world, China will remain in the primary stage of socialism for a long time to come. There remains significant room for progress in its human rights cause. Now that the country has fulfilled its first centenary goal, China has embarked on a new journey to build itself into a modern socialist country in all respects.

Standing at a new starting point in its development endeavors, China conforms to the people's aspirations for a better life and attaches even greater importance to respecting and protecting human rights. It is promoting coordinated progress in the economic, political, cultural, social and eco-environmental fields to meet the people's ever-growing need for multifaceted rights and beef up human rights protection in an all-round way. In today's world, poverty, wars and environmental problems, among others, have posed grave threats to human rights protection. The world is faced with prominent "governance deficit" in terms of human rights. To address these challenges, countries need solidarity instead of confrontation, cooperation instead of disengagement, openness instead of blockade, and communication instead of sanctions.

It is the common aspiration of human society that every one should enjoy human rights in the full sense of the term. To this end, countries should base their efforts on equality and mutual respect, actively engage in human rights dialogues and cooperation, expand consensus while bridging differences, learn from each other and pursue common progress, so as to make global governance of human rights fairer, more equitable, reasonable and inclusive, and deliver real benefits to people of all countries.

为了更加美好的世界

从人权视角看共建"一带一路"这十年

2023 年 12 月

前　言

2013年，中国国家主席习近平提出了共建"丝绸之路经济带"和"21世纪海上丝绸之路"，即共建"一带一路"倡议。共建"一带一路"旨在通过加强相关国家间全方位、多层面的交流合作，充分发掘、发挥各国的发展潜力和比较优势，形成互利共赢的利益共同体、责任共同体和命运共同体，实现以合作促发展，以发展促人权，促进共建国家共同发展繁荣，增进全人类福祉。

10年来，作为构建人类命运共同体的重要实践平台，共建"一带一路"已吸引了150多个国家和30多个国际组织参与，拉动近万亿美元投资规模，形成一大批合作项目，为共建国家创造众多工作岗位，帮助成千上万的民众摆脱贫困。10年来，共建"一带一路"从中国倡议走向国际实践，从理念转化为行动，从愿景转变为现实，成为当今世界深受欢迎的国际公共产品和国际合作平台，成为助力共建国家促进人权保障、实现美好生活的幸福之路。

促进和保障人权是全人类共同的事业。21世纪的今天，饥饿、贫困、战乱、环境污染等问题依旧存在，发展鸿沟不断拉大，不少国家还面临发展动能不足、总体发展水平偏低、基础设施落后等现实难题，这对人权发展与全球人权治理构成挑战。共建"一带一路"所体现的共同发展理念及所取得的实际成果，不仅为促进世界人权事业发展进步贡献了中国力量，也为完善全球人权治理贡献了中国智慧。

第一章

倡议实现共同发展，促进人人得享人权

　　发展是人类社会的永恒追求。唯有发展，才能消除冲突的根源，才能保障人民的基本权利，才能满足人民对美好生活的热切向往。发展中国家为了争取平等和公平的发展机会，提出了发展权的概念，发展权成为国际社会所公认的一项基本人权。

　　《世界人权宣言》强调"每个人……有权享受他的个人尊严和人格的自由发展所必需的经济、社会和文化方面各种权利的实现"。1986 年，联合国大会通过《发展权利宣言》，明确宣告发展权是不可剥夺的人权，"每个人和所有各国人民均有权参与、促进并享受经济、社会文化和政治发展，在这种发展中，所有人权和基本自由都能获得充分实现"。1993 年，世界人权大会通过《维也纳宣言和行动纲领》，再次强调发展权是一项普遍的和不可剥夺的权利，是基本人权的组成部分。2015 年，联合国通过了《2030 年可持续发展议程》，提出了贯彻落实发展权具体路径。

中国提出的共建"一带一路"倡议，顺应经济全球化的历史潮流，顺应全球治理体系变革的时代要求，顺应共建国家人民过上更美好生活的愿望期待，是共同发展的倡议，也是促进和保障人权的倡议。

1.1 共建"一带一路"：发展权实现的新路径新方案

当今时代，人类社会面临发展不平衡、不充分、不可持续等突出矛盾，以及饥饿、贫困、战乱、恐怖主义、环境污染、气候变化等诸多问题，给发展权的实现带来严峻挑战。如何破解这些难题？世界各国和国际社会都在进行深入思考和探讨。中国提出构建人类命运共同体理念，将共建"一带一路"作为推动实现各国共同发展和人民美好生活的实践平台，展现了共同面对全球性挑战，促进世界人权事业的大国责任和担当。

共建"一带一路"倡议是发展的倡议，为促进发展权的实现提供了现实路径和可行方案。共建"一带一路"把基础设施"硬联通"作为重要方向，把规则标准"软联通"作为重要支撑，把同共建国家人民"心联通"作为重要基础。通过政策沟通，形成政策协调、规划对接的合力，促进相关国家协同联动发展，不断夯实共建"一带一路"的政治基础；通过设施联通，以一系列重大项目和重点工作为引领，不断完善共建"一带一路"的基础设施网络；通过贸易畅通，促进贸易和投资自由化便利化，不断释放互利合作的活力；通过资金融通，深化金融领域合作，不断健全共建"一带一路"的多元化投融资体系；通过民心相通，搭建世界各国的友好桥梁，让共建"一带一路"更好造福世界各国人民。

共建"一带一路"倡议是中国为国际社会提供的一项充满东方智慧、有利于实现共同发展的全球公共产品。这一倡议倡导各方秉持共商、共建、共享原则，实现优势互补、互利共赢，为世界经济增长开辟了新空间，为国际贸易和投资搭建了新平台，为完善全球经济治理拓展了新实践，为增进各国民生福祉作出了新贡献，成为各国共同发展的机遇之路和繁荣之路。

1.2 共建"一带一路"：以合作促发展、以发展促人权的实践范本

共建"一带一路"，承载着人们对和平安宁的期盼、对共同发展的追求、对美好生活的向往、对文明交流的渴望，致力于让共建国家人民过上免于匮乏、获得发展、享有尊严的生活，这实质上与世界各国人民对于尊重和保障人权的不懈追求是完全一致的。

共建"一带一路"旨在以合作促发展，同联合国、东盟、

非盟、欧盟、欧亚经济联盟等国际和地区组织的发展和合作规划对接，同各国发展战略对接，在基础设施实现互联互通基础上开展金融、贸易、投资等各方面广泛合作，有效促进共同发展。世界银行研究报告显示，共建"一带一路"将使参与国贸易增长 2.8% – 9.7%、全球贸易增长 1.7% – 6.2%、全球收入增加 0.7% – 2.9%。联合国秘书长古特雷斯认为，共建"一带一路"倡议有助于推动经济全球化更加平衡、包容、和谐发展，对于通过国际合作解决当今世界面临的诸多挑战具有重大意义。

对大多数国家而言，消除饥饿和贫困、加快经济发展是最紧迫而现实的任务。共建"一带一路"倡议以发展促人权，积极帮助欠发达国家消除基础设施建设滞后等发展瓶颈，促进共建国家经济社会发展，在发展中保障和改善民生，不断夯实人权事业发展的根基，从而更好保护和促进人权。

1.3 共建"一带一路"为推进全球人权治理贡献了中国智慧

全球人权治理应该坚持民主协商原则。促进和保护人权是全人类的事业，不能由某个或某些国家说了算。共建"一带一路"倡议充分尊重各国主权安全、发展利益和文化传统，主张不同文明、不同国家相互尊重、相互包容、相互交流、相互借鉴，在完全自愿、充分沟通、求同存异和协商一致的基础上，开展政策对接和项目合作，彰显了"国际规则应该由各国共同书写"的理念。

全球人权治理应该坚持平等参与原则。各国无论大小、强弱、贫富，都是国际社会平等的一员，都能为完善全球人权治理贡献智慧和力量。共建"一带一路"倡议不是某个国家的"独奏曲"，而是各方的大合唱，坚持各国都是平等的参与者、贡献者、受益者，也是责任和风险的共同担当者，主张通过双边合作、第三方市场合作、多边合作等形式，鼓励更多国家和企业深入参与，持之以恒加以推进，契合了"全球事务应该由各国共同治理"的理念。

全球人权治理应该坚持合作共赢原则。面对战争冲突、金融危机、逆全球化和突发公共卫生事件给世界带来的种种不确定性，国际社会亟待加强合作，共同应对全球人权治理面临的严峻挑战。共建"一带一路"破除零和博弈思维，是中国同共建国家共享机遇、共谋发展的阳光大道，通过着力解决发展失衡、治理困境、数字鸿沟、分配差距等问题，让发展机会更加均等，让发展成果惠及广大民众，真正践行了"发展成果应该由各国共同分享"的理念。

第二章

让生命更有尊严：促进共建国家民众生存权的保障

生存权、发展权是首要的基本人权。共建"一带一路"通过一系列项目合作，促进各国经济社会发展，有效改善民众基本生活和医疗卫生条件、增加就业、提高收入水平，使民众的生存权得到更好保障。

2.1 助力满足基本生活需求

"民以食为天"。长期以来，饥饿是世界面临的最严重问题之一，在经济发展减缓和生态环境恶化的形势下，全球饥饿问题持续严峻。10 年来，在共建"一带一路"实施过程中，共建国家许多民众解决了饥饿和饮用水安全等问题，基本生活条件得到了改善。

农业合作是共建"一带一路"的重点领域之一。中国依据自身发展和减贫经验，助力共建国家农业生产，提高粮食产量，为当地民众消除饥饿创造条件。中国积极参与全球粮农治理，与相关国家发布《共同推进"一带一路"建设农业合作的愿景与行动》，与近90个共建国家和国际组织签署了100余份农渔业合作文件，建成中非农业科研机构"10+10"合作机制等区域农业合作长效机制，积极推动粮食安全区域合作。

从"吃不饱饭"到一家人丰衣足食并盖起了新房，布隆迪布班扎省农民夏尔·恩根达库马纳只用了4年。

"中国专家教会了我种植技术，让我有足够的粮食喂饱孩子们！"养育了7个孩子的夏尔说。自2018年起，他开始在中国专家指导下种植中国杂交水稻。如今日子好了，他家盖起了新房，在村里特别显眼。2023年，他还开办了一个大米加工坊，提高了经济回报，并为周围农户提供就业机会。

夏尔居住的吉汉加具宁加4村正是中国专家组在布隆迪设立的首个水稻减贫示范村。在中非合作论坛框架下，根据中布两国政府协议，中国自2009年8月起实施援布高级农业专家技术合作项目，累计有6批60人次中国农业技术专家赴当地执行援助任务，成功实施多个杂交水稻减贫示范村项目。中国专家深入田间地头开展调研和试验，引进多种适合当地种植的稻种，解决了山区水稻因稻瘟病减产甚至绝收的历史难题，并实现部分稻种本土化培育。布隆迪杂交水稻种植面积不断扩大，2023 年 6 月已达 4000 公顷，稻谷产量增加 1.9 万吨，农民收入增加 910 万美元，为实现布政府提出的"人人有饭吃、家家有积蓄"的愿景提供助力。

中国已向 70 多个国家和地区派出 2000 多名农业专家和技术人员，向多个国家推广示范 1500 多项农业技术，带动项目平均增产 40% 至 70%。

水是生命之源，但在全球不少地区特别是干旱地区，居民的基本生活用水仍常年得不到保障。乡村打井工程是中非落实"十大合作计划"的举措之一。塞内加尔邻近撒哈拉沙漠，中部和东部地区多为半沙漠地带，旱季最高气温可达 45℃。在远离城市的农村，村民基本生活用水十分困难。中方提供融资实施的乡村打井工程可解决塞内加尔七分之一人口的生活用水问题。

久尔贝勒区的泰内富勒村就曾是这样的一个缺水村落。"以前打水太难了，我们每天要步行 1.5 公里去邻村一口 25 米深的水井打水，排队时间有时从凌晨持续到午夜，村子里很多孩子因此都没法去上学。"村民迪昂说。

2018 年，中企打井项目组到泰内富勒村开始施工时，迪昂就进入施工队进行打井工作。水井落成后，迪昂被聘用为水井协调员，负责水井维护工作。迪昂说，现在自来水管接到了村里的家家户户，村民们在自家就能用到清洁的水，"这在以前是不敢想象的"。

正当迪昂的妻子用自家的水管接水做饭时，一群刚放学的小学生有说有笑地从门前路过。"现在有水了，孩子们能正常上学了，我们的生活也变好了。"迪昂说。

塞内加尔总统萨勒多次表示，乡村打井项目是塞"乡村发展紧急计划"的明星工程。打井供水项目遍及全国，意义重大，将真正为塞农业和农村地区发展提供强大支持。"我们感谢中国想塞内加尔之所想、急塞内加尔之所急，为该项目提供全面支持。"

2.2 促进实现工作权利

就业是最大的民生。共建"一带一路"通过一系列项目合作，为相关国家民众创造了更多的就业和培训深造机会，改善了当地人力资源状况。参与共建的中资企业充分保障属地员工在休息休假、医疗卫生等方面的权利。

在塞尔维亚，斯梅代雷沃钢铁厂5000余名员工因共建"一带一路"重获就业机会。这家曾被誉为"塞尔维亚的骄傲"的钢铁厂，关系着当地五分之一居民的生计，由于国际市场竞争激烈、管理不善等原因，一度陷入困境。2016年4月，中国河北钢铁集团收购这家钢铁厂，短时间内就实现扭亏为盈。

这家"重获新生"的钢铁厂，原有职工全部留用，中方只派遣了9名常驻管理人员。这一做法收获了当地员工的信任，也得到塞尔维亚政府的充分肯定。塞尔维亚总统武契奇说，中国企业挽救了这家濒临倒闭的钢铁厂，并保留了全部的工作岗位，加上与这家钢铁厂有合作关系的企业，一共可提供5万个就业岗位，这对塞尔维亚来说是个巨大的数字。

在老挝，中资民营公司亚钾国际2022年启动了"亚钾国际智慧产业园"项目，助力推动老挝工业化、城镇化发展进程，预计未来可为老挝每年增加3.2亿美元财政收入，带动就业3万至5万人。老挝政府总理宋赛·西潘敦表示，该公司项目是两国合作共赢的典范，为老挝经济社会发展提供了强劲动力，给当地人民带来了很多实惠。

中老铁路是老挝第一条现代化铁路，让老挝实现了"陆锁国"变"陆联国"的夙愿，不仅促进了区域互联互通和互利共赢，还带动了老挝当地的就业。自2021年12月3日开行以来至2023年5月，中老铁路累计招聘老挝员工3500多人，在物流、交通、商贸、旅游等行业间接增加就业岗位10万余个。得益于这条铁路，越来越多老挝山区的青年可以走出大山，拥抱世界。

在创造就业岗位的同时，中国企业还为属地员工提供培训深造机会，帮助员工提升能力素质。在希腊，中远海运比雷埃夫斯港口项目从2018年开始推出"教育资助金"计划，为在职深造的员工提供大部分学费支持。受该计划资助攻读工商管理硕士学位的中远海运港口比雷埃夫斯码头有限公司工程部主管安东尼斯·阿佩吉斯说："我对公司这种基于员工福祉的文化很满意。公司提供的良好工作环境以及我们从中获得的支持，使我们有能力应对未来挑战。"

在卡塔尔多哈，承建世界杯主体育场的中国铁建国际集团，不仅为来自 18 个国家的 3000 余名员工提供安全卫生的工作条件，还打造了建筑面积 5 万多平方米的"黄金等级"营地，礼拜室、洗衣房、体育设施、网吧等一应俱全，并为员工购买各类保险，配备专门医疗团队等，保障员工享有休息休假、社会保险和福利等各项权利。

2.3 提升居民收入水平

共建"一带一路"为共建国家创造了新的发展机遇，带动当地产业发展，助力当地居民增加收入、脱贫致富。

据世界银行研究报告，到 2030 年，共建"一带一路"将使相关国家 760 万人摆脱极端贫困、3200 万人摆脱中度贫困。

柬埔寨是共建"一带一路"的积极参与者，柬"五角战略"与"一带一路"倡议高度契合。在西哈努克省波雷诺县，作为"一带一路"中柬务实合作的样板工程，蓬勃发展的西哈努克港经济特区现已成为该省经济发展的"火车头"。经过多年持续建设发展，西港特区已有 175 家企业入驻，为近 3 万人解决了就业。西港特区内企业的年进出口总额超过 24 亿美元，特区工业产值对西哈努克省的经济贡献率超过 50%。

随着西港发展逐步迈上新台阶，大量游客、投资者来到西哈努克省，带动了当地旅游业、服务业、房地产业发展，当地人民获得了实实在在的好处。目前，西哈努克省的人均年收入已达到 4180 美元，在柬埔寨各省中位居第一，是全国平均水平的两倍以上。

新希望埃及有限公司是中国企业在埃及设立的全资子公司，旗下有 4 家饲料公司和 1 家种禽公司。公司从中国引进配方技术、生产管理体系和养殖服务体系，全球采购优质原料，通过优质产品、专业服务、产业配套、金融支持等体系化能力，每年带动当地养殖肉鸡量达 8500 万羽，每年为养殖户增加效益超 1.5 亿元。

一株"幸福草"，万家"致富路"。在卢旺达首都基加利的一家食用菌培育作坊里，工人们认真地将菌草粉、棉籽壳、石灰粉和水按比例混合，再经过消毒和包装，食用菌的培养皿菌袋就制作完成了。这家作坊的经营者埃马纽埃尔·阿希马纳，原本在当地一家糖厂担任机修工，常常为全家衣食烦心，后在中国专家指导下掌握了菌草技术。2016 年，阿希马纳创立了这家作坊，培育出的食用菌批发给当地菜市场、超市和餐厅，还远销到邻国乌干达和刚果（金）。

"利用菌草技术种植食用菌，在卢旺达现在可是一项利润丰厚的生意，这对人们摆脱贫困很有帮助。"阿希马纳说，"菌草技术带来的收入，除去孩子学费和生活开支，我还能存下一些资金继续扩大自己的生意。中国人的菌草技术，让我和其他很多人受益。"

在卢旺达，已有超过 3.5 万名农民接受了中国专家开设的菌草相关技术培训，3800 余户家庭、50 多家公司和合作社从事相关产业。目前，中国菌草技术已推广至全球 100 多个国家和地区，帮助不少农户脱贫致富。联合国经济和社会事务部国家战略和能力建设处处长阿姆松·西班达表示，菌草技术有助于实现消除贫困等多个可持续发展目标，已成为中国 – 联合国和平与发展基金的优先项目。

2.4 改善医疗健康条件

中国积极推动构建人类卫生健康共同体，在"一带一路"共建国家开展大量医疗援助和相关基建项目，为提高当地医疗服务水平、推动全球卫生健康事业发展作出贡献。

10 年来，中国持续向包括非洲、亚洲在内的全球数十个国家和地区派出医疗队，积极诊治患者，赢得广泛赞誉。目前，中国援外医疗队仍奋战在全球 56 个国家的 115 个医疗点，其中近一半在偏远和艰苦地区。

首例股骨头置换术、首例二尖瓣扩张分离术、首例断手再植术、首例脑外伤开颅术、首例角膜移植手术……多年来，中国医疗队在非洲各国创造了当地医疗史上的许多"首例"，用仁心仁术造福无数非洲患者，"中国医生"成为专业和可信任的代名词。

玛玛彻莉来自非洲南部国家莱索托一个偏远山村，长期承受着一种"怪病"的折磨——上腹和下腹各长出一个巨大的包块。由于当地医疗资源稀缺，加上病情复杂，虽然玛玛彻莉四处求医，但没有一家医院能收治她。

经多方打听，玛玛彻莉听说在莱索托北部莫特邦医院工作的中国医生可以帮助她。于是，她抱着试一试的心态，走了两三个小时的山路来到医院。经中国医疗队医生仔细检查，诊断玛玛彻莉的症状为"巨大子宫肌瘤合并上腹壁巨大疝"。经详细讨论研究和风险评估，医疗队将两次手术合并，一次性切除子宫联合腹壁巨大疝修补。当听到中国医生愿意并能够为她手术时，玛玛彻莉激动不已。

整个手术历时约 3 个小时，过程有惊无险，患者术后恢复也非常顺利，术后第二天就可以下床活动了。玛玛彻莉在手术成功后激动地说："谢谢中国医生，没有你们的帮助，我永远也无法摆脱这个怪病的折磨，你们是我的救命恩人！"

中国建设者为"一带一路"共建国家构筑健康防线添砖加瓦。2023 年 1 月，中国援非盟非洲疾病预防控制中心总部（一期）项目在埃塞俄比亚首都亚的斯亚贝巴竣工。项目建成后，将成为非洲大陆第一个拥有现代化办公和实验条件、设施完善的全非疾控中心。当地居民瓦克吉拉·托托法说："疟疾曾夺走了我亲人的生命，所以我从小对疾病充满了恐惧。听说项目竣工，我的亲朋好友们都很激动，这将改善我们的医疗条件。"

面对世纪疫情，中国致力于团结协作、携手抗疫，向120多个共建国家提供抗疫援助，向34个国家派出38批抗疫专家组，同31个国家发起"一带一路"疫苗合作伙伴关系倡议，向共建国家提供20余亿剂疫苗，与20余个国家开展疫苗生产合作，有力支持了"一带一路"共建国家抗击疫情。当中国医疗专家组抵达时，塞尔维亚总统武契奇亲赴机场迎接并深情献吻五星红旗；当中国援助的新冠疫苗运抵时，津巴布韦总统姆南加古瓦在总统府举行交接仪式。

第三章

让生活更有质量：推动共建国家民众发展权的实现

通过各种生产生活基础设施建设，共建"一带一路"在推动共建国家经济社会发展、助力满足当地居民基本生活需求的同时，倡导开展更广泛领域的合作，鼓励企业积极履行社会责任，帮助当地民众改善生活条件，更好实现教育、文化、环境等发展权利。

3.1 改善居民生活条件

基础设施建设是共建"一带一路"的重点内容，许多合作项目为当地民众提供了交通、通信、住房等各类设施和便利，帮助当地居民切实提高生活质量。

　　"朋友请听我讲，铁路的故事长又长。它凝结的是友谊，它带来的是希望。我的家乡，一天天更加美好；我的同胞，一天天更加昂扬……"肯尼亚歌手苏迪演唱的《蒙内之歌——铁路修到了我家乡》，讲述的正是由中企承建的肯尼亚蒙内铁路，歌中的铁路发展愿景正一一成为现实。

　　2017年5月31日，这条连接东非第一大港口蒙巴萨和首都内罗毕的标轨铁路建成通车。过去，两地间乘坐长途汽车通常需要10小时以上，价格高、耗时长的旅途让旅客身心俱疲，如今乘坐蒙内铁路直达列车只需4个多小时，便捷与舒适感不言而喻。蒙内铁路通车后，内罗毕居民莉莲·奥图玛踏上前往蒙巴萨海边度假的旅程。她说，这是她第一次乘坐现代化的列车，方便快捷的蒙内铁路帮她实现了多年的愿望。

　　截至2023年9月30日，蒙内铁路已安全运营2314天，累计发送旅客1115.5万人次，平均上座率达95.8%，单日旅客最高发送量突破1万人次；累计运输240.5万个标箱，发送货物2860.9万吨。据肯尼亚铁路局估算，该项目对肯国内生产总值贡献率超过2%。

　　2016年4月至5月间，厄瓜多尔连续发生强烈地震，造成重大人员伤亡和财产损失。中国第一时间伸出援手，积极支持厄方灾后重建。厄政府设立的"居者有其屋"全国保障房项目同样得到了中方支持，现已有不少市民入住新房。与两个年幼孩子一起生活的西尔维娅·马卡斯说："感谢中国给了我们一个家，让我和孩子们可以过上有尊严的生活。"

近年来，中国数字基建项目"多点开花"，促进了互联互通和无缝贸易，改善了当地民众生活面貌。2021 年底，泰国以诗里拉吉医院为试点启动 5G 智慧医院项目。该项目引进中国华为的 5G、云和人工智能等技术，从 5G 救护车入院、人工智能辅助诊断到出院后的远程医疗，助力医院服务流程实现全面智能化转型。诗里拉吉医院院长威实表示，5G 救护车为救治节省了时间，大大提高了急救病人的存活率。

类似的例子不胜枚举：截至 2021 年 11 月，中国企业建设了非洲 50% 以上无线站点及高速移动宽带网络，累计铺设超过 20 万公里光纤，服务超过 9 亿非洲民众；在南非建立了服务非洲地区的公有"云"，以及首个 5G 独立组网商用网络；中国云技术进入拉丁美洲市场以来，大大推动了该地区数字化发展，助力当地技术创新。

3.2 提升教育水平

人人都有受教育的权利。在"一带一路"建设中，中国与合作伙伴一道努力让当地居民有更多受教育的机会，学习专业知识、掌握专业技能，助力当地改善教育条件、提升教育水平。

2017 年，秘鲁遭遇严重洪灾和泥石流灾害，许多学校严重损毁，中国企业积极参与灾后重建。2022年10月，中国电力建设集团承建的4所学校全部交付使用。其中一所学校的校长布斯塔曼特女士说："看到学校面貌焕然一新，学生回到具备抗震能力及功能完善的校园，我非常激动，对建设者们表达衷心感谢。"

2022年底，在巴布亚新几内亚首都莫尔兹比港布图卡学园首届高三班毕业典礼上，巴新首都行政区长官鲍维斯·帕科普表示，布图卡学园的建设是中国发展惠及全球的生动例证。"每名学生都是巴新和中国教育合作的受益者。"

布图卡学园是中方为当地出资援建的惠民工程，自2018年11月启用后，成为莫尔兹比港新地标。该学园原来是一所拥有1500名学生、建筑面积为2000平方米的小学，部分教室由于年久失修已经坍塌，课桌椅严重不足，很多学生只能坐在地上听课。扩建后的学园建筑面积达10800平方米，涵盖幼儿园、小学、中学等共计52个班，解决了3000多名中小学生的上学难问题，成为巴新国内面积最大、功能最齐全、设施最先进的学校。

葡萄牙塞图巴尔理工学院自动化专业学科带头人约瑟·卢卡斯教授至今仍记得与天津同行的"初次相见"。2018年，他第一次来到天津机电职业技术学院时，就被学院实训设备与技术的先进性深深震撼，"我从没想到中国的技术已经发展到世界领先水平"。

中葡在先进技术的教育合作上硬件、软件互补。中方侧重设备实操安装，而葡方侧重系统调试。"一拍即合，是一个相互成就的过程。"深度参与葡萄牙鲁班工坊建设的天津机电职业技术学院电气自动化教研室主任姜颖这样形容两所学校的合作。

"在这里，我不仅学会了使用各种机器人、视觉设备等，还开发了一个工业通信研究项目。"塞图巴尔理工学院学生亚历山大·热拉尔多在葡萄牙鲁班工坊学习实训3年来收获颇丰。

2022年8月，首届世界职业院校技能大赛在天津举行，来自100多个国家和地区的千余名师生参赛，其中就包括天津机电职业技术学院的何琳峰、张博师生与葡萄牙鲁班工坊的索萨、路易斯·巴罗索师生组成的队伍。

虽然由于疫情不能见面，但队友们克服时差，同步"云端"备赛。"每周都会连线好多次，每一个细微的难题都要共同研究、解决，在互相学习的过程中，我们凝聚成了一个整体，成了亲密的伙伴。"张博说。最终，这个团队获得了智能产线安装与调试赛项银牌。

2016年以来，中国院校与亚非欧三大洲的20多个共建国家院校合作建设一批鲁班工坊，开设工业机器人、新能源、物联网等专业，开展学历教育累计3300余人，培训规模超1.2万人，为当地培养大批本土化技术技能人才。

3.3 支持公共文化建设

享受文化成果，参与文化活动，是文化权利的重要体现。共建"一带一路"许多项目在实施中，积极参与公共文化基础设施建设，保护挽救当地文化遗产，丰富了共建国家文化资源，助力当地民众文化权利的实现。

中国援非"万村通"项目旨在让非洲国家 1 万个村庄收看到卫星数字电视。截至 2022 年底，"万村通"项目已顺利在非洲 21 个国家落地，覆盖非洲 9512 个村落，直接受益家庭超过 19 万户，覆盖民众近千万。从用不上电，到看上卫星数字电视，该项目的非洲本地员工埃米尔说："当我们有了'眼睛'之后，也就有了了解世界和改变家园的工具，可以了解到更加先进的发展技术和发展模式。"

2022 年 5 月，中远海运比雷埃夫斯港口有限公司与希腊文化和体育部在比港举行场地出让签约仪式，中方企业将提供约 1.3 万平方米的场地，用于建设希腊水下考古博物馆，丰富港口文化内涵和当地民众文化生活。

"我愿出一袋黄金，只求看一眼希瓦。"这句中亚古语所说的乌兹别克斯坦千年古城希瓦，曾因城内部分古建筑年久失修，这颗丝路"明珠"一度蒙尘。得益于中乌联合修复项目以及中国专家的匠心巧思，如今的希瓦古城恢复了原有风貌，再次绽放光彩。希瓦古城伊钦·卡拉内城博物馆馆长沙基尔·马达米诺夫说："中国专家对希瓦古城的修复工作持续了3年，现在古城变得非常美丽。看到修复后的古城，这里的居民都非常骄傲，因为这是乌兹别克斯坦的文化瑰宝。"

3.4 尊重宗教习俗

宗教信仰自由是一项基本的人权。风俗习惯是一个国家或民族广大民众在历史长河中所创造、享用和传承的生活文化。在共建"一带一路"过程中，中方充分尊重各国民众宗教信仰和风俗习惯，为当地的宗教场所建设提供服务或资金支持，为当地员工进行宗教和民俗活动提供便利。

雅万高铁是中国和印尼发展战略对接和共建"一带一路"的旗舰项目。为尊重当地民众的宗教信仰和印尼的文化传统，中方设计团队为印尼量身打造方案。据介绍，雅万高铁站房设计因地制宜，采用传统与现代相结合的理念，充分融合印尼当地宗教和文化特点，体现当地人文元素，站房内设置了穆斯林专用祈祷室等设施。在项目建设中，中国企业为中方员工培训宗教礼仪等内容，并在开斋节、宰牲节等节日向当地员工和周边清真寺等赠送礼物。

由中国建筑集团有限公司承建的阿尔及尔大清真寺，是非洲最大、世界第三大清真寺，已成为当地新地标，并被印上了阿尔及利亚的纸币。当地居民哈布勒·纳迪尔说，阿尔及尔大清真寺是现代伊斯兰建筑的典范，通过到这里参加宗教活动，他可以结识更多的穆斯林，分享彼此感受和经历，从而更好地理解自己的宗教信仰。

3.5 保护生态环境

"一带一路"不仅是经济繁荣之路，也是绿色发展之路。中国始终致力于推进共建"一带一路"绿色发展，尊重各国民众的环境权，遵守当地相关法律法规，构建生态环保合作平台，推动当地实现经济社会和生态环境协调发展，让绿色成为共建"一带一路"的底色。

中国积极推动建立共建"一带一路"绿色低碳发展合作机制，与联合国环境规划署签署《关于建设绿色"一带一路"的谅解备忘录》，与有关国家及国际组织签署 50 多份生态环境保护合作文件。与 31 个共建国家共同发起"一带一路"绿色发展伙伴关系倡议，与 32 个共建国家共同建立"一带一路"能源合作伙伴关系。发起建立"一带一路"绿色发展国际联盟，成立"一带一路"绿色发展国际研究院，建设"一带一路"生态环保大数据服务平台，帮助共建国家提高环境治理能力、增进民生福祉。积极帮助共建国家加强绿色人才培养，实施"绿色丝路使者计划"，已为 120 多个共建国家培训 3000 人次。制定实施《"一带一路"绿色投资原则》，推动"一带一路"绿色投资。

由中国承建的肯尼亚蒙内铁路运营以来，沿线蒙巴萨红树林湿地公园中的红树林茂盛如常。这得益于中方工程团队施工期间在红树林生长范围预埋多处过水管涵，确保海水能够进入被施工便道隔断的区域以浸润红树林，让其正常生长。此外，蒙内铁路在全线设置多处动物通道，并采用声屏障技术降低列车通过时的噪音。肯尼亚著名环保人士阿里·穆罕默德说："我为我的国家有这样一条现代化铁路感到自豪，因为它不仅助力经济振兴，更重视保护沿线生态，项目方所做努力保护了包括红树林在内的海洋生态系统。"

中国科学院新疆生态与地理研究所、中亚生态与环境研究中心与哈萨克斯坦林业委员会、塞富林农业技术大学共同实施哈萨克斯坦首都圈生态林建设技术示范项目，建立百亩苗圃并开展种植技术和灌溉培训。在项目实施中，中哈双方组建了联合考察团队，考察了多种防护林带，共同梳理建设障碍因子。中方邀请哈方多位专家到新疆考察当地的生态工程，在植物选择、结构配置、初植密度控制等方面共同商定意见。双方共同努力，攻克了高抗逆植物选育、规模化育苗等多项关键技术，突破了干旱坡地、砾质荒地等困难立地造林的技术瓶颈，构建了林带抚育管护技术方案，创建了亚寒带荒漠草原造林技术模式，建立了监测网络。目前，该项目已建设完成 20 多公顷固碳示范防护林，助力构建哈国首都圈生态防护屏障，减轻了草原大风天气对居民生活的影响。

中国企业还努力帮助当地民众提高环保意识。中国港湾工程有限责任公司在参与投资、建设、运营尼日利亚莱基港过程中，经常向属地员工和周边村民普及环保知识，开展海滩垃圾清理等活动。2022年6月，公司与当地环保协会联合举办"海滩拯救行动"，300余名周边村民与公司员工共同清理了约5平方公里的海滩。非洲海洋可持续发展协会主席法利西亚说："中国公司的行动充分证明，他们不仅遵守当地法律法规，而且高度重视环境保护。他们努力帮助当地民众提高环保意识，与合作伙伴共同保护环境。"

第四章

让发展更加普惠：推动特定群体平等共享共建成果

共建"一带一路"，努力促进各国妇女、儿童、老年人、残障人士等特定群体权益的保障，使其能平等地参与社会生活，共享"一带一路"发展成果。

4.1 促进妇女权益保障

平等就业，保障妇女的经济权利，是提高妇女社会和家庭地位、实现男女平等的关键。

2016 年 4 月，巴基斯坦信德省政府、多家巴方企业和中国机械设备工程股份有限公司组成联营体，开始建设塔尔煤田露天煤矿项目，需要大量翻斗车司机。项目部全部启用巴方司机，建立专门培训基地，累计培训上万人次，其中包括 50 多名女性。女性司机的聘用不仅为家庭增加了收入，还提升了女性社会地位。

努斯拉特·巴伊原是巴基斯坦塔尔地区巴格尔县的一名裁缝，生活窘困，经过一年培训，成了优秀的翻斗车司机，每月的薪酬是之前的十几倍。"我现在是县里少数能买得起牛奶、水果和好衣服的人了。全家生活发生巨大变化，简直难以用言语来表达我的幸福！"

莫西尼·巴伊是一位 4 个孩子的母亲，以前没有工作，一家人的生活只能依靠做小贩的丈夫，她非常渴望被聘为一名翻斗车司机。然而，按当地习俗，没有兄弟或丈夫的陪同，女性很难单独外出工作。"项目上为了支持我，把我丈夫也招进来了。现在我们俩都在项目上工作，工资很丰厚，孩子们也能上学了，我们正在盖一座漂亮的砖房。"莫西尼说。

在菲律宾吕宋岛，中国电力建设集团有限公司圣马塞利诺光伏发电项目部主动优化施工步骤，特地分出预装螺栓、分拣垫片等适合女性的工作，为附近村庄的妇女提供了近百个就业岗位。不少当地女工直言，这份工作不仅增加了收入，而且让她们看到了自身价值，家庭地位也明显提升。

改善女性就医条件，提高女性健康水平。在肯尼亚南部承接大坝项目的中国能建葛洲坝集团，在了解到当地一所医院不仅没有专门的产科病房，而且缺少相关设施后，出资建起了一座妇产楼，为孕产妇和新生儿提供了良好的医疗健康服务条件。

4.2 关注儿童权益

儿童是世界的未来和希望。在共建"一带一路"中，中国企业通过捐资助学、改善设施、志愿活动，努力促进儿童权益的实现，使儿童成为共建"一带一路"的重要受益者。

伊拉克曾拥有中东地区最好的教育条件，但多年战乱冲突导致校舍短缺，许多学生只能在简易板房或改装后的集装箱里上课。为解决"上学难"问题，伊拉克政府制定新建学校规划，并将其列为最紧迫的民生工程之一。在首期招标的1000所学校中，中国电建承建了其中10个省份的679所，项目建成后将解决约43万名学生的上学问题。

2018年1月，中柬双方签署《关于开展"爱心行"项目的谅解备忘录》，决定帮助救治柬埔寨先天性心脏病患儿。此后，来自中柬两国的医务人员深入柬埔寨10多个省份的偏远乡村，筛查数万名儿童。患有先天性心脏病的柬埔寨男孩杜当成了受益者之一，经过两国医务人员通力合作，杜当顺利在云南省阜外心血管病医院接受免费手术并恢复了健康。

2021年11月，中国第19批援塞内加尔医疗队抵达塞内加尔，在迪亚姆尼亚久儿童医院开展为期2年的援外医疗任务，中国医生的精湛医术和强烈责任心受到当地民众的高度评价和普遍赞扬。截至 2023 年 3 月 31 日，医疗队完成门诊 7058 人次，手术 3150 台次。

2022 年 5 月 23 日，在"六一"国际儿童节到来之际，中建埃及分公司联合 4 家驻埃中资企业一同前往埃及非洲难民儿童学校"非洲希望就学中心"，向孩子们赠送教材书籍、学习文具、儿童口罩等物品。埃及非洲难民儿童学校行政助理埃梅卡·艾德敏表示，这将有助于改善所有学生的学习条件，为难民儿童带来一个更美好的未来。

类似的故事还有很多。在柬埔寨，在多家中国企业的帮助下，柬埔寨儿童艺术福利院有了新的校舍、厨房、卫生间，老旧的设备设施得以更新换代……

4.3 关心残疾人权益

共建"一带一路"是一个包容发展的大平台，在促进共建国家经济社会发展的同时，也关注到了残疾人这个特殊的群体，帮助其发挥技能所长，使其成为共建"一带一路"的参与者、受益者。

在巴基斯坦，华能公司积极聘用当地残疾人，为其提供平等就业机会。公司从建设初期就开始在生活区和工作区打造了无障碍出入通道和电梯等设施，为残疾员工提供低楼层宿舍，帮助他们更好地融入集体，实现梦想和价值。

公司高级财务经理穆罕默德·卡希夫因幼时患病致双腿无法行走，但始终坚信腿部的残疾绝不会阻碍自己实现人生理想。自加入华能公司以来，他凭借优秀的工作能力和职业素养，帮助公司不断完善税制建设，积极争取税收优惠，向当地税务机关展示了公司的良好形象，连续多年获得先进个人称号。

2022 年的一天，温暖的阳光照进秘鲁一所崭新的幼儿园，患有神经退行性疾病的小女孩雅米蕾正开心地坐在教室里，又一次朗诵起她喜爱的诗歌。5 岁的雅米蕾因患病无法行走，此前主要靠老师抱着上下楼梯。现在雅米蕾坐着由中国电建捐赠的电动轮椅，可以通过电梯和无障碍通道上下楼，洗手间也设有无障碍设施，这对像雅米蕾这样的残疾学生来说非常便利。

在希腊中部帕尔纳索斯滑雪中心，40 岁的高山滑雪运动员乔治·斯法尔托斯使用定制的坐姿滑雪器，为争取拿到 2026 年米兰－科尔蒂纳丹佩佐冬残奥会的入场券而努力训练。

参加冬残奥会是斯法尔托斯的梦想。但因无力承担新设备的费用，斯法尔托斯的训练计划深受影响，他一度丧失希望。在寻求社会支持的过程中，中远海运港口比雷埃夫斯码头有限公司向他伸出了援手：公司捐赠了一套为他定制的坐姿滑雪器。"这为我追逐梦想提供了真切的帮助。"斯法尔托斯说，"通过竞技体育，我一点点找到了自己的立足点，我会继续追逐我的梦想。"

第五章

共建"一带一路"对全球人权治理的启示

当前，世界不公正、不容忍、不安宁的状况依然存在，发展不平衡、不协调、不可持续的问题依旧突出，世界人权事业发展和全球人权治理面临严峻挑战，人类亟须探索符合时代要求的全球人权治理理念与方案。

共建"一带一路"顺应广大发展中国家希望通过合作发展促进人权的迫切期许，助力共建国家的经济社会发展和人权进步，为全球人权治理提供了新思维、新动力、新机遇。

5.1 以民为本

人民幸福生活是最大的人权。一国人权状况好不好，关键看本国人民的利益是否切实得到维护，人民的获得感、幸福感、安全感是否得到增强。

共建"一带一路"坚持以人民为中心的发展思想，聚焦消除贫困、增加就业、改善民生，让共建成果更好惠及各国人民，为当地经济社会发展和人权事业进步作出实实在在的贡献。10年来，150多个共建国家秉持合作共赢的理念，通过共建"一带一路"持续推动经济社会文化发展，不断提升人民生活品质、增进民生福祉。

人权不是一部分人或少数人享有的特权，而是所有人平等享有的权利。正如瑞典"一带一路"研究所所长史蒂芬·布劳尔所指出，"一个至关重要的理念是实现所有人的共同利益"，从这个意义上说，共建"一带一路"与人权事业发展的目标是一致的，同构建人类命运共同体是契合的。

全球人权治理应坚持以民为本。以人民为中心的人权理念蕴含人类文明价值追求，符合联合国将人权纳入国际治理体系、促进所有人的人权和基本自由的初衷，尊重世界各国人民对美好生活的向往；代表人权事业发展的前进方向，使人权更加真实、全面，为世界人权发展注入全新内涵。

5.2 合作发展

各项人权相互依赖不可分割是人权保护的基本原则，同时对于占全球人口80%以上的发展中国家而言，生存权、发展权显得尤为重要而迫切。没有发展奠定物质基础和各方面社会条件，人类其他权利的实现都是非常困难甚至不可能的。在各国发展深度交融的今天，合作共赢是破解发展困局、扫除发展障碍的最优解。通过加强合作保障人民生存和发展，通过经济社会的全面发展来带动其他人权的渐进式保护，对广大发展中国家乃至世界人权事业发展具有重要启示意义。

《维也纳宣言和行动纲领》强调，"国际社会应促进有效的国际合作，实现发展权利，消除发展障碍"。共建"一带一路"搭建起了包容、务实的广泛国际合作平台，其和平合作、互利共赢的理念吸引了世界上超过四分之三的国家和30多个国际组织加入其中，它能有效激活共建国家的经济发展潜力，促进共建国家经济社会发展，契合了国际社会"以合作促发展，以发展促人权"的现实诉求，符合推动完善全球人权治理的时代需要。

法国席勒研究所国际问题专家塞巴斯蒂安·佩里莫尼认为，共建"一带一路"从不是中国一家独奏，而是共建国家的合唱协奏，中国以合作促发展，共建"一带一路"为全球共同发展作出了重要贡献，中国的倡议有利于实现合作共赢，这是当今世界应该选择的正确道路。

5.3 开放包容

人权是历史的、具体的、现实的。各国国情不同，历史文化、社会制度、经济社会发展水平存在差异，面对的人权问题不尽相同，应坚持将人权的普遍性原则与各国实际相结合，走适合本国国情的人权发展道路，根据本国实际确定人权的优先选择、保障方式和实现途径。各国应以平等开放的精神维护文明的多样性，加强不同文明的对话和交流，通过对话交流凝聚更多共识，共同推动人权发展进步。

共建"一带一路"坚持相互尊重、平等相待，倡导文明宽容，尊重各国自主选择的发展道路和模式，尊重彼此核心利益和重大关切，客观理性看待别国发展壮大和政策理念，努力求同存异、共谋发展。

印度尼西亚《雅加达邮报》网站刊文指出，共建"一带一路"跨越了不同的国家和地区，不同的文化和宗教，不同的习俗和生活方式。在共建"一带一路"下，共建国家所秉持的共同目标，是寻求建立互惠互利的伙伴关系。

5.4 公平公正

全球人权治理应弘扬和平、发展、公平、正义、民主、自由的全人类共同价值，维护各国人民的尊严和权利，推动构建人类命运共同体，共同开创世界美好未来。各国体量有大小、国力有强弱、发展速度有快慢，但都是国际社会平等的一员，都有平等参与包括人权在内的地区和国际事务的权利。

共建"一带一路"跨越不同地域、不同发展阶段和不同文明，从不带任何文明优越感，不排除也不针对任何一方，对共建国家的政治经济制度不附加特殊要求，各共建国家在发展过程中享有权利公平、机会公平、规则公平，是平等的参与者、贡献者、受益者，休戚与共、命运相连。共建"一带一路"秉持的"共商、共建、共享"原则，摒弃了一些国家面对不同文化和文明要么征服要么同化的强权逻辑，努力推动构建一个更加公平、公正的秩序规范。

发展人权是全人类的事业。世界唯有将"你""我""他"变成"我们"，让每个国家和每个国家的人民都享有平等的权利和机会，才能有效应对全球挑战，真正实现平等参与、合作共赢，共享人权发展成果。

结 语

　　共建"一带一路"倡议源自中国，更属于世界；根植于历史，更面向未来。

　　共建"一带一路"的第一个 10 年，是中国与各国在国际合作新范式下共同发展的 10 年，也是在共同发展中保障和增进人权的 10 年。

　　当前，世界又一次站在历史的十字路口。构建人类命运共同体是世界各国人民前途所在。只有各国平等互利、合作共赢、共同发展，繁荣才能持久，人人充分享有人权的伟大梦想才能实现。

　　我们相信，在共建"一带一路"的下一个 10 年，中国将继续以自身新发展为世界提供新机遇，为推动构建人类命运共同体增添新动能，中国人民与各国人民必将因此享有更加广泛、更加充分、更加全面的权利，在更高水平上实现全面发展。

For a Better World

Looking at the past decade of jointly pursuing the
'Belt and Road' Initiative from a human rights perspective

December 2023

Introduction

In 2013, Chinese President Xi Jinping proposed the joint construction of the "Silk Road Economic Belt" and the "21st Century Maritime Silk Road," known as the "Belt and Road" Initiative (BRI). The BRI aims to enhance all-dimensional and multi-tiered exchanges and cooperation among relevant countries, fully tap into and leverage each country's development potential and comparative strengths, and create a community of shared interests, shared responsibility, and shared destiny. It seeks to promote development through cooperation and human rights through development to advance the joint development and prosperity of partner countries and enhance the well-being of all humanity.

Over the past decade, as a crucial practical platform for building a community with a shared future for humanity, the BRI has attracted participation from more than 150 countries and over 30 international organizations. It has driven investment of nearly one trillion dollars, generated a multitude of cooperative projects, created numerous job opportunities for partner countries, and helped lift thousands upon thousands of people out of poverty. Over the past decade, the BRI has become a highly popular international public good, a global cooperation platform, and a path to happiness, aiding partner countries in promoting human rights protection and achieving a better life.

Promoting and safeguarding human rights is a common cause for all of humanity. Today, in the 21st century, hunger, poverty, conflicts, and environmental pollution persist while the development gap continues to widen. Many countries still face practical challenges like insufficient development momentum, relatively low overall development performance, and outdated infrastructure, which challenge the development of human rights and global human rights governance. The vision of common development and actual achievements embodied in the Belt and Road cooperation have contributed to China's strength in advancing the global human rights cause and offered Chinese wisdom for improving global human rights governance.

Chapter 1

Initiatives Aiming to Achieve Common Development and Promote the Enjoyment of Human Rights for All

Development is the eternal pursuit of human society. Only through development can we address the root causes of conflicts, safeguard the people's fundamental rights, and meet their aspirations for a better life. Developing countries have put forth the concept of the right to development to seek equal and fair development opportunities, and the right to development has become a universally recognized fundamental human right in the international community.

The Universal Declaration of Human Rights emphasizes that "Everyone, as a member of society, has the right to social security and is entitled to realization, through national effort and international co-operation and in accordance with the organization and resources of each State, of the economic, social and cultural rights indispensable for his dignity and the free development of his personality." In 1986, the United Nations (UN) General

Assembly adopted the Declaration on the Right to Development, clearly proclaiming that the right to development is an inalienable human right, stating that "The right to development is an inalienable human right by virtue of which every human person and all peoples are entitled to participate in, contribute to, and enjoy economic, social, cultural and political development, in which all human rights and fundamental freedoms can be fully realized." In 1993, the World Conference on Human Rights adopted the Vienna Declaration and Programme of Action, reiterating that the right to development is a universal and inalienable right and an integral part of fundamental human rights. In 2015, the UN adopted the 2030 Agenda for Sustainable Development, outlining a concrete pathway for implementing the right to development.

The cooperative construction of the "Belt and Road" Initiative proposed by China conforms to the historical trend of economic globalization, the requirements of the times for the transformation of the global governance system, and the strong desire of people of partner countries to live a better life. It is an initiative for common development and for promoting and protecting human rights.

1. Jointly pursuing the "Belt and Road" Initiative provides new paths and approaches to achieve the right to development

In today's era, humanity faces prominent issues of unbalanced, inadequate, and unsustainable development and many problems like hunger, poverty, war, terrorism, environmental pollution, and climate change, which pose severe challenges to realizing the right to development. How do we tackle these thorny problems? Countries worldwide and the international community have been exploring ideas to answer the question. China has put forward the concept of building a community with a shared future for humanity, using the joint pursuit of the BRI as a practical platform to promote the common development of all countries and uplift the living standard of their people. The concept demonstrates a major country's responsibility for addressing global challenges and advancing the cause of human rights worldwide.

Joint pursuit of the BRI is a development initiative that provides realistic paths and feasible plans for promoting the realization of the right to development. It takes the "hard connectivity" in infrastructure as an important direction, "soft connectivity" in rules and standards as an essential support, and "heart connectivity" with the people of the partner countries as a vital foundation. We will continue consolidating the political foundation of cooperative construction of the BRI to promote coordinated development among partner countries by creating synergy for policy communication and planning connectivity through policy coordination. Guided by major projects and critical undertakings, we will continue improving the jointly built BRI's infrastructure network through facility connectivity. We will continue unleashing the vitality of mutually beneficial cooperation by promoting trade and investment liberalization and facilitation through unimpeded multilateral trade. We will continue enhancing the jointly built BRI's diversified investment and financing system to further collaborate in the financial sector through financial connectivity. We will make the BRI's cooperative construction better benefit the people of all countries and achieve people-to-people connectivity by building friendly bridges among nations worldwide.

The joint pursuit of the BRI is a global public good offered by China to the international community, characterized by Eastern wisdom and conducive to achieving common development. This initiative advocates the principles of consultation, cooperation, and shared benefits, aiming to achieve complementarity and mutual benefit. It has opened up new opportunities for global economic growth, established new platforms for international trade and investment, expanded new practices for improving global economic governance, and made new contributions to enhancing the well-being of people in all countries, thus becoming a path of prosperity for the common development of all nations.

2. Jointly pursuing the "Belt and Road" Initiative provides a practical model for promoting development through cooperation and advancing human rights through development

The joint pursuit of the BRI embodies people's aspirations for peace and tranquility, their pursuit of common development, their longing for a better life, and their desire for cultural exchange. It is committed to ensuring that people from partner countries can live a life free from deprivation, enjoy development, and have dignity. In essence, this aligns perfectly with the unwavering pursuit of respecting and protecting human rights by people worldwide.

The cooperative construction of the BRI aims to promote development through cooperation. It aligns with the development and cooperation plans of international and regional organizations such as the United Nations, ASEAN, the African Union, the European Union, the Eurasian Economic Union, and various countries' development strategies. It fosters extensive finance, trade, and investment cooperation by building upon infrastructure connectivity, effectively promoting common development. According to a World Bank research report, participation in the BRI is expected to increase trade among partner countries by 2.8% to 9.7%. UN Secretary-General Antonio Guterres believes that the cooperative construction of the BRI contributes to more balanced, inclusive, and harmonious development in economic globalization. It holds significant importance for addressing the many challenges facing the world today through international cooperation.

For the majority of countries, the most urgent and practical task is to eliminate hunger and poverty and accelerate economic development. Joint pursuit of the BRI promotes human rights through development, actively assisting underdeveloped countries in overcoming development bottlenecks such as infrastructure deficits, fostering the economic and social development of co-building nations, ensuring and improving people's livelihoods in the process of development, continually strengthening the foundation of human rights development, and thereby better protecting and promoting human rights.

3. Jointly pursuing the "Belt and Road" Initiative has contributed Chinese wisdom to advancing global human rights governance

Global human rights governance should adhere to the principle of democratic consultation. Promoting and protecting human rights is a universal endeavor that one or a few countries should not determine. The cooperative construction of the BRI fully respects all nations' sovereignty, security, development interests, and cultural traditions. It advocates mutual respect, inclusivity, exchange, and learning among various civilizations and countries. The initiative encourages engagement in development policy synergy and cooperative projects through voluntary participation, open communication, and seeking common ground while preserving differences and reaching consensus through negotiation. It reflects the idea that "international rules should be written together by all."

The principle of equal participation should be upheld in global human rights governance. Regardless of their size, strength, or wealth, all countries are equal members of the international community and can contribute wisdom and strength to improving global human rights governance. Joint pursuit of the BRI is not one country's solo performance but a symphony played by all partners. It emphasizes that all parties involved in jointly pursuing the BRI are equal participants, contributors, and beneficiaries and that they are also shared bearers of responsibilities and risks. It advocates for increased participation through various forms of cooperation, including bilateral, third-party market, and multilateral cooperation, encouraging more countries and enterprises to engage in and profoundly and persistently advance the initiative. It aligns with the idea that "global affairs should be jointly handled by all."

The principle of win-win cooperation should be adhered to in global human rights governance. Faced with various uncertainties brought about by war conflicts, financial crises, anti-globalization trends, and sudden public health emergencies, the international community urgently needs to strengthen cooperation to address the grave challenges facing global human rights governance. Jointly pursuing the "Belt and Road" rejects zero-sum thinking and provides a sunshine road for China and partner countries to share opportunities and seek development together. Focusing on addressing issues such as development imbalances, governance challenges, the digital divide, and income disparities ensures more equal development opportunities by allowing development benefits to reach a broader population. It embodies the idea that "development benefits should be shared by all."

Chapter 2

Enhancing Dignity of Life: Promoting the Protection of the Right to Life for the People of the "Belt and Road" Partner Countries

The rights to subsistence and development are the primary, basic human rights. The BRI, through a number of cooperative projects, promotes the economic and social development of various countries, effectively improving people's basic living and healthcare conditions, increasing employment, and raising income levels, thereby better ensuring their right to sustenance.

1. Facilitating the satisfaction of basic life necessities

The Chinese see "food as an overriding priority." Hunger has long been one of the most severe problems facing the world. Amid slowing economic development and a deteriorating ecological environment, the global issue of hunger continues to be a grave problem. Over the past decade, many people in partner countries have solved the issues of hunger and drinking water safety by jointly pursuing the BRI. As a result, their fundamental living conditions have improved.

Agricultural cooperation is one of the critical areas of the cooperative construction of the "Belt and Road." Drawing upon its experience of development and poverty reduction, China has assisted partner countries in agricultural production, increasing their food production and creating conditions to alleviate hunger among local populations. China actively participates in global food and agricultural governance and has jointly released the "Vision and Action on Jointly Promoting Agricultural Cooperation along the Belt and Road" with relevant countries. China has signed over 100 agricultural and fishery cooperation documents with nearly 90 partner countries and international organizations. It has also established regional agricultural cooperation mechanisms, such as the "10+10" cooperation mechanism for Sino-African agricultural research institutions, actively promoting regional cooperation in food security.

Charles Ngendakumana, a farmer from the Bubanza Province, Burundi, went from not having enough to eat to providing his family with plenty of food and building a new house in just four years.

"Chinese experts taught me planting techniques, allowing me to have enough food to feed my children!" said Charles, a father of six. He started growing Chinese hybrid rice four years ago under Chinese experts' guidance. Today, the yield from his land has increased from less than 6 tons per hectare to 9 tons, and the cultivation area has expanded from half a hectare to five.

"As livelihood improved, his family has built a new house that stands out in the village. "Next, I plan to buy more land and a few more cows and add two new water pumps when the dry season comes," Charles envisions for the future.

The Ninga 4 Village, Commune of Gihanga, where Charles resides, is the first rice-based poverty reduction demonstration village established by a

Chinese expert team in Burundi. Under the framework of the China-Africa Cooperation Forum and based on agreements between the governments of China and Burundi, China has implemented a high-level agricultural expert technical cooperation project in Burundi since August 2009. A total of five batches of 45 Chinese agricultural technology experts have been sent to the region to assist with aid tasks. They have successfully implemented several demonstration village projects on hybrid rice and poverty reduction. Chinese experts conducted in-depth field research and experiments, introducing various rice varieties suitable for local cultivation. They solved historical challenges in mountainous areas where rice crops suffered from reduced yields or even complete losses due to the disease of rice blast fungus (Magnaporthe grisea). They also achieved the localized cultivation of some rice varieties. The cultivation area of hybrid rice in Burundi has been continuously expanding, reaching 4,000 hectares by June 2023. Rice production has increased by 19,000 tons, and farmers' incomes have grown by 9.1 million US dollars. This progress contributes to the Burundian government's vision of "food for all and savings for every household."

As of 2021, China had sent more than 2,000 agricultural experts and technicians to more than 70 countries and regions, promoted and demonstrated more than 1,500 agricultural technologies in many countries, and helped projects increase production by 40% to 70% on average.

Water is the source of life, but residents' access to essential drinking water remains unsecured year-round in many regions worldwide, especially in arid areas. The Rural Well Project is one of the measures under the China-Africa "Ten Major Cooperation Plans." Senegal, located near the Sahara Desert, has vast central and eastern areas that are semi-desert zones, with temperatures reaching as high as 45°C during the dry season. In rural areas far from cities, villagers face significant challenges in basic drinking water. After implementing the Rural Well Project, financed by China, 251 wells will be sunk, and 1,800 kilometers of pipelines will be laid. This initiative will address the water needs of one-seventh of Senegal's population.

Touba Fall in the Diourbel Region was once such a water-scarce village. "Fetching water used to be very difficult for us. We had to walk 1.5 kilometers daily to a neighboring village to draw it from a well 25 meters deep. Sometimes, we had to line up from early morning till midnight. Many children in the village had to miss school," said Dioung, one of the villagers.

In 2018, when the Chinese companies' well-digging project team arrived at the village of Touba Fall, Dioung joined the team to work on sinking a well. After completing the well project, Dioung was hired as the well's coordinator, responsible for its maintenance. Dioung mentioned that now, water pipes have reached every household in the village, enabling the villagers to have access to clean water right in their homes. He said "it was unimaginable in the past."

While Dioung's wife was cooking with the water from the pipe system, a group of elementary school students walked by, chatting and laughing. Dioung remarked "now that we have water, the children can attend school regularly, and our lives have improved as well."

Macky Sall, president of Senegal, has repeatedly stated that the Rural Well Project is a flagship initiative under Senegal's the Urgent Community Development Program. The well-sinking and water-supply project spans the country, holds significant importance, and will provide robust support for developing agriculture and rural areas in Senegal. "We are thankful that China has aligned its priorities with those of Senegal and provided comprehensive support to this project," he added.

2. Promoting the realization of the right to work

Employment is the cornerstone of people's livelihoods. The BRI, through a number of collaborative projects, has created more jobs and provided more vocational training and education opportunities for the people in partner countries, thereby improving their human resource situation. Chinese companies involved in the BRI fully ensure the rights of their local employees in terms of rest, holidays, healthcare, and more.

In the Smederevo Steel Plant in Serbia, over 5,000 employees found new job opportunities through their involvement in the BRI. Once known as "Serbia's pride," this plant had supported the livelihoods of one-fifth of the local population but faced difficulties due to intense international market competition and mismanagement. In April 2016, China's Hebei Iron and Steel Group acquired the steel plant and turned it around from losses to profits in a short period.

This "reborn" steel plant retained all its original employees, with only nine Chinese resident managers sent by the Chinese side. This approach earned the trust of the local workers and received full recognition from the Serbian government. Serbian President Aleksandar Vucic stated that the Chinese company saved this nearly bankrupt steel plant and preserved all its jobs. Together with the cooperating businesses, this steel plant can provide 50,000 job opportunities, a significant number for Serbia.

The Chinese private company Asia Potassium International launched the "Asia Potassium International Smart Industry Park" project in Laos in 2022, contributing to advancing its industrialization and urbanization. It is expected to increase Laos' annual fiscal revenue by 320 million US dollars and generate employment for 30,000 to 50,000 people. Lao Prime Minister Sonexay Siphandone stated that this project is a model of win-win cooperation between the two countries, providing a strong impetus for Laos' economic and social development and bringing many benefits to the local people.

The China-Laos Railway is Laos' first modern railway, fulfilling the country's long-standing aspiration to transform from a "landlocked country" to a "land-linked country." It has not only promoted regional connectivity and mutual benefits but has also generated employment opportunities in Laos. From its commencement on December 3, 2021, to May 2023, the China-Laos Railway recruited over 3,500 Laotian employees and indirectly created more than 100,000 jobs in logistics, transportation, trade, and tourism. Thanks to this railway, an increasing number of young people from remote areas of Laos can step out of the mountains and embrace the world.

While creating job opportunities, Chinese companies also provide training and educational support to local employees, helping them enhance their skills and qualifications. In Greece, the COSCO Shipping Piraeus Port project launched the "Educational Assistance Fund" program in 2018, providing significant tuition support for employees pursuing further education while working. Antonis Apergis, the engineering department supervisor, is seeking a Master's in Business Administration with the program's assistance. He said, "I am very pleased with the company's culture that prioritizes employees' well-being. The excellent working environment provided by the company and the support we receive have empowered us to tackle future challenges."

In Doha, Qatar, China Railway International Group, which built the World Cup main stadium, not only provides safe and sanitary working conditions for over 3,000 employees from 18 different countries but has also established a "gold-level" camp with a construction area of more than 50,000 square meters. This camp includes the amenities of prayer rooms, laundromats, sports facilities, and internet cafes. In addition, the company purchases various insurances for the employees, equips them with a dedicated medical team, and ensures they enjoy rights such as vacation time, social insurance, and fringe benefits.

3. Raising the income levels of people

The BRI has created new development opportunities for partner countries to drive local industrial development, helping residents increase their income and lifting them out of poverty.

According to a research report by the World Bank, by 2030, the BRI is expected to lift 7.6 million people in partner countries out of extreme poverty and 32 million people out of moderate poverty.

Cambodia actively participates in the BRI, and its "Five Pillar Strategy" aligns well with the initiative. In Preah Sihanouk province, as a model project for practical cooperation between China and Cambodia under the BRI, the thriving Sihanoukville Special Economic Zone has become the economic driver of the province's development. After years of continuous construction and development, the economic zone has attracted 175 companies, employing nearly 30,000 people. The annual import and export volume of enterprises in the special economic zone exceeds 2.4 billion US dollars, contributing more than 50% of the province's economic output.

With Sihanoukville's continual progress, many tourists and investors have come to Preach Sihanouk province, driving the development of the local tourism, service, and real estate sectors, benefiting the local population directly. Currently, the per capita annual income in Preah Sihanoukville Province has reached 4,180 US dollars, ranking first among all the provinces in Cambodia and more than double the national average.

New Hope Egypt Limited Company is a wholly-owned subsidiary of a Chinese enterprise established in Egypt, with four feed companies and one poultry breeding company under its umbrella. The company has imported formulation technology, production management systems, and breeding service systems from China, while sourcing high-quality raw materials globally. Through systematic capabilities in high-quality products, professional services, industry support, and financial assistance, it annually supports the local poultry farming industry with a production of 85 million broilers and increases poultry farmers' income by over 150 million RMB.

One "happiness fungus" plant leads to prosperity for thousands of families. In a mushroom cultivation workshop in the capital city of Kigali, Rwanda, workers carefully mix Juncao powder, cottonseed husks, lime powder, and water in the proper proportions. After sterilization and packaging, bagged mushroom culture dishes are ready. Emmanuel Ashimana, the operator of this workshop, used to work as a mechanic in a local sugar factory and was often concerned about his family's livelihood. However, with the guidance of Chinese experts, he mastered the mushroom substrate technology. In 2016, Ashimana founded this workshop, where the cultivated mushrooms are wholesaled to local vegetable markets, supermarkets, and restaurants and exported to neighboring countries like Uganda and the Democratic Republic of Congo.

"Using Juncao technology to cultivate mushrooms is now a lucrative business in Rwanda. And it's helping people escape poverty," said Ashimana. "I have four children, and with the income generated from Juncao technology, I can even save some money to expand my business further after covering my children's school fees and our living expenses. The Chinese Juncao technology has benefited me and many others."

In Rwanda, over 35,000 farmers have received Juncao Technology-related training provided by Chinese experts, and more than 3,800 households, along with over 50 companies and cooperatives, are engaged in related industries. Currently, Chinese Juncao Technology has been extended to over 100 countries and regions worldwide, helping many farmers escape poverty. Amson Sibanda, Chief of the National Strategies and Capacity Building Branch in the Division for Inclusive Development, UN Department of Economic and Social Affairs, noted that Juncao Technology contributes to achieving various sustainable development goals, making it a priority project for the China-United Nations Peace and Development Fund.

4. Improving healthcare conditions

China actively promotes the construction of a human health community and carries out a large number of medical assistance and related infrastructure projects in countries participating in the BRI, contributing to improving the level of local medical services and promoting the development of global health undertakings.

Over the past decade, China has continued to send medical teams to dozens of countries and regions around the world, including Africa and Asia, and has actively diagnosed and treated patients, winning widespread praise. Currently, Chinese foreign aid medical teams are still working at 115 medical points in 57 countries worldwide, nearly half of which are in remote areas with harsh living conditions.

Over the years, Chinese medical teams have achieved many "firsts" in the medical history of various African countries, such as the first hip replacement surgery, the first mitral valve separation surgery, the first hand-reattachment surgery, the first craniotomy for traumatic brain injury, and the first corneal transplant surgery. Their compassionate care and expertise have benefited numerous African patients, and the "Chinese Docs" have become synonymous with professionalism and trustworthiness.

Mamacherie comes from a remote mountain village in Lesotho, a country in southern Africa. She has been suffering from a "strange disease" for a long time: a massive lump in her upper and lower abdomen. Due to the scarcity of local medical resources and the complexity of her condition, Mamacherie sought medical treatment everywhere, but no hospital could treat her.

Mamacherie heard that Chinese doctors working at Motebang Hospital in Northern Lesotho could help her. So, with the attitude of giving it a try, she walked two or three hours on the mountain road to the hospital. After careful examination by doctors from the Chinese medical team, Mamacherie's symptoms were diagnosed as "huge uterine fibroids combined with a huge hernia in the upper abdominal wall." After a detailed discussion and risk assessment, the medical team combined the two operations into a one-time hysterectomy and repair of the sizable abdominal wall hernia. Mamacherie was excited when she heard that Chinese doctors were willing and able to operate on her.

The entire surgery took approximately three hours, and the procedure went smoothly without complications. The patient's postoperative recovery was also very successful, and she could get out of bed and move around on the second day after surgery. Mamacherie, in her exhilaration after the successful surgery, exclaimed "thank you, Chinese doctors. Without your help, I would have never been able to escape the torment of this strange illness. You are my lifesavers!"

Chinese builders contribute to creating a robust health defense system in the Belt and Road Initiative partner countries. In January 2023, Phase I of the Chinese-aided African Union Africa CDC Headquarters project was completed in Addis Ababa, the capital of Ethiopia. After completion, it will become the first modern and well-equipped African CDC on the continent, offering office space and advanced laboratory facilities. Local resident Wakjira Totofa expressed that "Malaria has taken away the lives of my loved ones, so I have always feared diseases. When I heard about the completion of this project, my family and friends were all very excited. It will improve our medical conditions."

In the face of the century's worst pandemic, China is committed to unity and cooperation, joining hands with the world community in the fight against COVID-19. China has sent 38 batches of expert teams to 34 countries and provided over 2.2 billion vaccine doses to more than 120 countries and international organizations, offering vital support to BRI partner countries in their fight against the pandemic. When Chinese medical expert teams arrived, Serbian President Aleksandar Vucic greeted them at the airport, warmly kissing the five-star red flag. When Chinese-assisted COVID-19 vaccines arrived in Zimbabwe, President Emmerson Mnangagwa held a handover ceremony at the presidential palace.

Chapter 3

Improving the Quality of Life: Promoting the Realization of the Right to Development of the People in the "Belt and Road" Partner Countries

Through constructing various production and life infrastructures, the cooperative construction of the BRI promotes partner countries' economic and social development, helps meet their residents' basic needs, and advocates for broader cooperation in various fields. It encourages companies to fulfill their social responsibilities actively, assisting local communities in improving living conditions and realizing their rights to development in areas such as education, culture, and the environment.

1. Improving living conditions

Infrastructure development is a key focus of cooperatively building the "Belt and Road" with many collaborative projects providing various facilities and conveniences such as transportation, communication, and housing for local populations. These initiatives help residents significantly improve their quality of life.

"My friend, please listen to my long story of the railway.

It cements friendship, and it brings hope.

My hometown is more beautiful day by day,

My compatriots are more high-spirited day by day...."

These are the lyrics from the "Song of the Mombasa-Nairobi Railway - A Railway to My Hometown," sung by Kenyan artist Sudi Boy, telling the story of the Mombasa-Nairobi Standard Gauge Railway (SGR) built by Chinese companies. The vision of railway development depicted in the song is becoming a reality one by one.

On May 31, 2017, this SGR connecting the largest port in East Africa, Mombasa, with the capital, Nairobi, was completed and opened for operation. In the past, traveling between these two cities by long-distance bus often took over 10 hours, with high costs and a lengthy journey that left passengers exhausted. Today, passengers can reach their destination on the Mombasa-Nairobi Railway in just over four hours, enjoying its convenience and comfort. After the railway's opening, Nairobi resident Lilian Otuma embarked on a journey to the seaside in Mombasa. She mentioned that it was her first time riding a modern train, and the convenient and fast Mombasa-Nairobi Railway fulfilled her dream for many years.

Having operated without major hitches for 2,314 days as of Sept. 30, 2023, the modern railway line stretching from Mombasa to Naivasha had transported 2,405 million standard containers and 28.609 million metric tons of goods since its reception.

The number of passengers transported through the Mombasa-Nairobi-Naivasha SGR in the same period stood at 11.155 million, with an average seat occupancy rate of 95.8 percent.

Between April and May 2016, Ecuador experienced a series of strong earthquakes that resulted in significant loss of life and property. China promptly extended a helping hand and actively supported Ecuador in post-disaster reconstruction efforts. The Ecuadorian government's "Housing for All" national housing project also received support from China, and many citizens have since moved into new homes. Silvia Marquez, who lives with her two young children, expressed her gratitude by saying "thanks to China, we have a home where my children and I can lead a dignified life."

In recent years, China's digital infrastructure projects have achieved results in many areas, promoting connectivity and seamless trade to improve the lives of local populations. At the end of 2021, Thailand launched a 5G Smart Hospital project with Siriraj Hospital as the pilot site. This project introduced technologies such as 5G, cloud computing, and artificial intelligence from China's Huawei Technologies Co., Ltd. It facilitated the comprehensive digital transformation of hospital services, from 5G ambulance services to AI-assisted diagnostics and remote healthcare for discharged patients. Dr Visit Vamvanij, the director of Sriraj Hospital, stated that 5G ambulances have saved crucial time in treating patients and significantly improved survival rates for emergency cases.

Examples like this abound. As of November 2021, Chinese companies have constructed over 50% of wireless sites and high-speed mobile broadband networks in Africa, laying over 200,000 kilometers of optical fiber and providing services to over 900 million African people. A public "cloud" serving the African region and the first commercial standalone 5G network has been established in South Africa. Introducing Chinese cloud technology into the Latin American market has significantly driven regional digital development and supported local technological innovation.

2. Enhancing education standards

Everyone has the right to education. In the BRI, China and its partner countries strive to provide more educational opportunities for their residents, enabling them to acquire professional knowledge and skills, thereby improving their education conditions and standards.

In 2017, Peru experienced severe flooding and mudslides, which caused significant damage to many schools. Chinese companies actively participated in post-disaster reconstruction efforts. In October 2022, Power Construction Corporation of China completed the construction of four schools. Mrs. Bustamante, the principal of one of these schools, said, "I am very excited to see the school completely renovated and students returning to campus with earthquake-resistant features and improved functionality. I want to express my heartfelt gratitude to the builders."

At the end of 2022, during the graduation ceremony of the first senior class at Butuka Academy in Port Moresby, the capital of Papua New Guinea, Mr. Powes Parkop, Governor of the National Capital District of Papua New Guinea, stated that the establishment of Butuka Academy serves as a vivid example of China's development benefiting the world. He emphasized that every student benefits from the educational cooperation between Papua New Guinea and China.

A Chinese-funded project for the local community, Butuka Academy, has been built by China to benefit the local people. Since its inauguration in November 2018, it has become a new landmark in Port Moresby. The academy was originally a primary school with 1,500 students and a building area of 2,000 square meters. Some classrooms collapsed due to disrepair, and there was a severe shortage of desks and chairs, forcing many students to sit on the floor during classes. After expansion, the academy now covers an area of 10,800 square meters and includes facilities for kindergarten, elementary, and middle school education, totaling 52 classrooms. This expansion has successfully addressed the challenges more than 3,000 primary and secondary students face in accessing education. It has become the largest, most comprehensive, and most advanced school in Papua New Guinea in terms of its facilities and functionality.

Professor Jose Pedro Magalhaes Lucas, the leading expert in automation at the Polytechnic Institute of Setubal in Portugal, still vividly recalls his first encounter with colleagues from Tianjin. In 2018, during his initial visit to the Tianjin Vocational College of Mechanics and Electricity, he was profoundly impressed by the college's advanced training equipment and technology. "I never imagined that China's technology is leading the world," he remarked.

Where advanced technology education is concerned, Sino-Portuguese collaboration thrives on a hardware-software synergy. The Chinese side excels in equipment operation and installation, while the Portuguese strength lies in system debugging. "It's a perfect match, a mutually enriching process," describes Jiang Ying, the Director of the Electrical Automation Research Department at Tianjin Vocational College of Mechanics and Electricity, deeply involved in establishing the Luban Workshop in Portugal.

"Here, I not only learned how to use various robots and machine vision but also developed an industrial communication research project." Alexander Geraldo, a student at the Polytechnic Institute of Setubal, has gained a lot during his three years of practical training at the Luban Workshop in Portugal.

In August 2022, the first World Vocational College Skills Competition was held in Tianjin. Over a thousand teachers and students from more than 100 countries and regions participated, including a team of students and teachers from Tianjin Vocational College of Mechanics and Electricity and the Luban Workshop in Portugal. The former pair comprised He Linfeng and Zhang Bo, and the latter, Sosa and Luis Barroso.

Although they could not meet in person due to the pandemic, the teammates overcame the time difference and synchronized their preparations in the "cloud." "We connect multiple times weekly and jointly research and resolve every challenge no matter how minute. We became a cohesive unit and developed close bonds through learning from each other," said Zhang Bo. Ultimately, this team won the silver medal in the intelligent production line installation and debugging competition.

Since 2016, China has established more than 20 "Lu Ban Workshops" in countries participating in the BRI. These workshops offer programs in industrial robotics, new energy, the Internet of Things (IoT), and other specialized fields. They have provided formal education to over 3,300 individuals and conducted training for more than 12,000 people. This initiative has contributed significantly to developing a substantial number of skilled technical professionals in these regions.

3. Supporting public cultural development

Enjoying cultural achievements and participating in cultural activities are important manifestations of cultural rights. Many projects of joint pursuit of the BRI are being implemented, actively participating in constructing public cultural infrastructure, protecting and salvaging local cultural heritage, enriching partner countries' cultural resources, and helping their people realize cultural rights.

The Chinese "Access to Satellite TV for 10,000 African Villages" project aims to provide satellite digital television access to 10,000 villages in African countries. As of the end of 2022, the project has successfully been implemented in 20 African countries. It covers 9,512 villages, benefiting over 190,000 households of nearly ten million people. Transitioning from having no access to electricity to being able to watch satellite digital television, Emir, a local employee of the project in Africa, said: "When we gained "eyes," we also acquired tools to understand the world and improve our homeland. We can now learn about more advanced development technologies and models."

In May 2022, China COSCO Shipping Corporation Limited's Piraeus Port Authority (PPA) signed an agreement with the Greek Ministry of Culture and Sports in the Port of Piraeus. According to the agreement, the Chinese company will provide approximately 13,000 square meters of land to construct the Underwater Archaeology Museum of Greece to enhance the port's cultural significance and enrich the local community's cultural life.

"I am willing to give a bag of gold just to catch a glimpse of Khiva," says this ancient saying from Central Asia. The thousand-year-old city of Khiva in Uzbekistan had some of its ancient buildings in disrepair due to the passage of time, causing this "pearl" of the Silk Road to be "covered in dust" for a while. Thanks to the joint restoration project between China and Uzbekistan and the ingenious craftsmanship of Chinese experts, the ancient city of Khiva has now been restored to its original appearance and is once again shining brightly. Shakir Madaminov, the director of the Ichan-Kala Museum-Reserve, stated, "Chinese experts have been involved in restoring the ancient city of Khiva for three years, and now the city looks exceptionally beautiful. Seeing the restored ancient city, the residents here are very proud because it is a cultural treasure of Uzbekistan."

4. Respecting religious customs

"Freedom of religious belief is a fundamental human right and a long-standing basic policy of the Chinese government. Customs and habits represent the cultural heritage created, enjoyed, and passed down by the vast populations of a nation or ethnic group throughout history. In jointly constructing the BRI, China fully respects the religious beliefs and customs of the people in various countries, provides services or financial support for the construction of local religious venues, and facilitates local employees to carry out religious and folk activities.

The Jakarta-Bandung High-Speed Railway is a flagship project of China and Indonesia to foster greater synergy between development strategies and the BRI's joint pursuit. To respect Indonesia's local population's religious beliefs and cultural traditions, the Chinese design team tailored its plan for the project. It is reported that the design of the Jakarta-Bandung High-Speed Railway station buildings is adapted to the local context, following the concept of combining traditional and modern elements and fully integrating the religious and cultural characteristics of Indonesia to incorporate local cultural elements. The station buildings include facilities such as dedicated prayer rooms for Muslims. Chinese companies trained their employees on religious etiquette and related matters during the project's implementation. They also gift local employees and nearby mosques during festivals like Eid al-Fitr and Eid al-Adha.

The Great Mosque of Algiers, constructed by China State Construction Engineering Corporation (CSCEC), is the largest mosque in Africa and the third-largest in the world. It has become a new landmark and is featured in Algerian currency. A resident named Habib Nadir mentioned that the Great Mosque of Algiers exemplifies modern Islamic architecture. By attending religious activities here, he can meet more fellow Muslims to share experiences and feelings, thus better understanding his people's religious beliefs.

5. Protecting the ecological environment

The BRI is a path not only to economic prosperity but also to green development. China has consistently been committed to promoting green development within the framework of the joint pursuit of the BRI. This commitment involves respecting the people's environmental rights in partner countries, adhering to local laws and regulations, establishing platforms for ecological and environmental cooperation, and fostering harmonious economic, social, and ecological development in the local areas. This approach aims to make green development a fundamental aspect of the joint pursuit of the BRI.

China is actively promoting the establishment of a cooperative mechanism for green and low-carbon development for the joint pursuit of the BRI. They have signed the Memorandum of Understanding on Green Belt and Road Construction with the UN Environment Programme (UNEP) and have entered into more than 50 cooperation agreements on ecological and environmental protection with relevant countries and international organizations. China has jointly launched the Initiative for Belt and Road Partnership on Green Development with 31 partner countries and jointly established the Belt and Road Energy Partnership with 32 partner countries. It also launched the BRI International Green Development Coalition, established the Green Belt and Road Lab, and set up the BRI Environmental Big Data Platform. These initiatives aim to help partner countries enhance their environmental governance capabilities and improve the well-being of their populations. China is actively assisting partner countries in strengthening green talent development by implementing the "Green Silk Road Ambassador Program," which has trained over 3,000 people from more than 120 partner countries. Additionally, they have formulated and implemented the "Green Investment Principles for the Belt and Road" to promote green investments in the BRI.

Since the Mombasa-Nairobi Standard Gauge Railway (SGR) constructed by China began to operate, the mangrove forests in the Mombasa Mangrove Wetland Park along the railway line have continued to thrive as usual, thanks to the efforts of the Chinese engineering team. During the SGR's construction, China pre-installed multiple water culverts within the mangrove growth area to ensure that seawater can enter the area cut off by construction work to nourish the mangroves and allow them to grow undisturbed. Additionally, many sections of the SGR run through wildlife passages. Therefore, sound barrier technology has been applied to reduce noise when trains pass through. Renowned Kenyan environmentalist Ali Mohammed commented, "I am proud that my country has such a modern railway because it not only contributes to economic revitalization but also prioritizes the protection of the ecosystem along the route. The efforts made by the project have safeguarded marine ecosystems, including the mangrove forests."

The Xinjiang Institute of Ecology and Geography, the Chinese Academy of Sciences, and the CAS Research Center for Ecology and Environment of Central Asia, in collaboration with the Forestry and Wildlife Committee of the Ministry of Agriculture of Kazakhstan and the S. Seifullin Kazakh AgroTechnical University jointly implemented the Kazakhstan Capital Region Ecological Forest Construction Technology Demonstration Project. They established a nursery spanning hundreds of acres and provided training in planting techniques and irrigation. During the project's implementation, a joint survey team from China and Kazakhstan examined various protective forest belts and collectively identified construction obstacles. China invited several Kazakh experts to inspect ecological projects in Xinjiang, and together, they reached agreements on plant selection, structural configuration, and initial planting density control. They overcame critical technical challenges through concerted efforts, including selecting highly stress-resistant plants and large-scale seedling cultivation. They also broke through technical bottlenecks for afforestation on arid slopes and gravelly barren land. They developed forest belt nurturing and maintaining techniques, created a reforestation model for subarctic desert grasslands, and established monitoring networks. As of now, the project has completed more than 20 hectares of demonstrative carbon-sequestration protection forests, contributing to establishing an ecological protective barrier for the capital region of Kazakhstan and mitigating the impact of grassland windstorms on its residents' lives.

Chinese companies also make efforts to raise environmental awareness among local communities. During their involvement in the investment, construction, and operation of the Lekki Port in Nigeria, China Harbour Engineering Company Limited regularly educates local employees and nearby villagers about environmental protection and conducts activities such as beach cleanups. In June 2022, the company collaborated with a local environmental association to organize a "Beach Rescue Action" event involving over 300 villagers from the surrounding area and company employees. Together, they cleaned approximately 5 square kilometers of the beach. Dr Felicia Chinwe Mogo, President of the African Marine Environment Sustainability Initiative (AFMESI), commented, "The Chinese companies' actions demonstrate that they not only adhere to local laws and regulations but also prioritize environmental protection. They work diligently to raise environmental awareness among local communities and collaborate with partners to protect the environment."

Chapter 4

Making Development More Universally Beneficial: Guaranteeing Special Groups' Equal Access to the Results of the Cooperative Construction of the "Belt and Road"

In the joint pursuit of the BRI, efforts are being made to promote the protection of the rights and interests of special groups, including women, children, the elderly, and persons with disabilities from various countries, aiming to enable them to participate equally in social life and share the benefits of developing the joint pursuit of the BRI.

1. Promoting the protection of women's rights and interests

Equal employment and safeguarding women's economic rights are key factors in improving women's social and family status and achieving gender equality.

In April 2016, the Sindh government of Pakistan, several Pakistani companies, and China Machinery Engineering Corporation (CMEC) formed a consortium to initiate the construction of the Thar Coal Field's open-pit mining project, which required a significant number of dump truck drivers. The project employed exclusively Pakistani drivers, establishing a dedicated training center that provided training to tens of thousands of individuals, including over 50 women. The employment of female drivers not only increased household income but also enhanced the social status of women.

Nusrat Bai, originally a tailor in Bhakuo of the Thar district, faced financial hardship. After a year of training, she became an outstanding dump truck driver, earning several times more monthly than before. She said, "Now, I'm one of the few in my area who can afford milk, fruit, and good clothes. Our family's life has changed tremendously, and it's hard to describe how happy I am."

Mosini Bai is a mother of four children who had no prior employment. Her family's livelihood depended solely on her husband's small vendor business. She had a strong desire to work as a dump truck driver. However, according to local customs, it was nearly impossible for women to work independently without the companionship of brothers or husbands. She said, "The project also hired my husband to support me. Now, both of us are working on the project, and we receive a good income. Our children can go to school, and we are building a beautiful brick house,' Mosini added.

On the island of Luzon, the Philipines, the Powerchina International Group Limited Office of the San Marcelino Photovoltaic Power Project actively optimized the construction process by creating specific tasks suitable for women, such as pre-installing bolts and sorting washers. This initiative has provided nearly a hundred job opportunities for women in nearby villages. Many local female workers have expressed that this job increased their income, made them recognize their worth, and significantly improved their status in their families.

China is committed to improving healthcare conditions for women to enhance their health. China Gezhouba Group Company Limited, which undertook a dam project in southern Kenya, learned that a local hospital lacked a dedicated maternity ward and essential facilities. Therefore, they invested in constructing a maternity building, providing pregnant women and newborns with improved healthcare services.

2. Paying attention to children's rights and welfare

Children are the future and hope of the world. In the BRI, Chinese companies strive to push for the realization of children's rights through donations for education, infrastructure improvement, and volunteer activities, thereby ensuring that children become the BRI's essential beneficiaries.

Iraq once had the best educational facilities in the Middle East, but years of conflict and turmoil have resulted in a shortage of school buildings. Many students can only attend classes in makeshift huts or converted shipping containers. To address the "access to education" challenge, the Iraqi government has formulated plans for new school construction, prioritizing it as one of the most urgent projects for the well-being of its citizens. In the first phase, out of the 1,000 schools tendered, Powerchina International Group Limited has been contracted to construct 679 schools in ten provinces. Upon completion, this project will provide access to education for approximately 430,000 students.

In January 2018, China and Cambodia signed the "Memorandum of Understanding of the 'Love Heart Journey' Project," aiming at providing medical assistance to children with congenital heart disease (CHD) in Cambodia. Subsequently, medical professionals from the two countries conducted screenings in remote villages across more than ten provinces in Cambodia, examining tens of thousands of children. One of the beneficiaries of this program was a Cambodian boy named Doudang suffering from CHD. Through the collaborative efforts of medical personnel from both countries, Doudang successfully underwent free surgery and fully recovered at the Fuwai Hospital in Yunnan Province, China. The hospital is also China's National Center for Cardiovascular Diseases.

In November 2021, the 19th batch of Chinese medical teams arrived in Senegal, starting a two-year medical assistance mission at the Chinese-aided Children's Hospital of Diamniadio. The Chinese doctors' remarkable medical skills and a strong sense of duty received high praise and widespread acclaim from the local population. As of March 31, 2023, the medical team had conducted outpatient services for 7,058 patients and performed 3,150 surgeries.

On May 23, 2022, a few days before the International Children's Day, the China State Construction Engineering Corporation's Egypt branch, in collaboration with four other Chinese enterprises in Egypt, visited the "African Hope Learning Center" for refugee children to provide them with textbooks, stationery, and children's masks. Emeke Adim, the Administrative Assistant at the center, expressed that this initiative would help improve the learning conditions for all students and contribute to a brighter future for refugee children.

Similar stories abound. Take Cambodia for example, again. With the help of Chinese enterprises, the Cambodian Children's Art Welfare Institute boasts a new school building with kitchens and bathrooms, and its outdated equipment and facilities have been upgraded...

3. Caring for the rights of disabled individuals

The cooperative construction of the BRI is a significant platform for inclusive development. While promoting partner countries' economic and social development, it also pays attention to the special group of persons with disabilities, helping them hone their skills and making them participants and beneficiaries of the joint pursuit of the BRI.

In Pakistan, China Huadian Group Co., LTD. hires local individuals with disabilities, providing them with equal employment opportunities. It built accessible pathways and elevators in residential and work areas when construction began. They also accommodate employees with disabilities on the ground floor of their dormitories, helping them better integrate into the community and realize their dreams and values.

Mr. Mohammad Kashif, the senior financial manager of the company, cannot walk due to an illness he suffered in his childhood. Still, he always believed that his physical disability would never hinder him from achieving his life goals. Since joining China Huadian Group, he has constantly helped the company improve its tax system with his excellent competency and professionalism. He works hard to pursue tax incentives and demonstrate the company's positive image to local tax authorities. As a result, he has received the title of "Outstanding Individual" for multiple consecutive years.

One day in 2022, warm sunlight streamed into a brand-new kindergarten in Peru, where a little girl named Yamile, who suffered from a degenerative neurological condition, sat happily in her classroom, reciting her favorite poem once again. Five-year-old Yamile, who could not walk due to her illness, had previously been carried up and down the stairs by her teachers. Thanks to an electric wheelchair donated by Powerchina International Group Limited, Yamile could navigate the building using elevators and accessible pathways. The restrooms also feature disability-friendly facilities, making it much more convenient for disabled students like Yamile.

At the Parnassos Ski Resort in the central part of Greece, 40-year-old alpine skier George Sfaltos is diligently training with a customized sit-ski, trying to earn a spot at the 2026 Winter Paralympics taking place in Milan and Cortina d'Ampezzo, Italy.

Participating in the Winter Paralympics is George Sfaltos' dream. However, due to the inability to afford new equipment, Sfaltos' training plans were severely impacted, causing him to lose hope. In his quest for social support, China COSCO Shipping Corporation Piraeus Port Authority SA (PPA) extended a helping hand by donating a customized sit-ski for him. "The act has provided tangible assistance for me to pursue my dream," said Sfaltos. "I have found my footing little by little through competitive sports. I will continue to chase my dream."

Chapter 5

The Relevancy of the Joint Pursuit of the "Belt and Road" Initiative for Global Human Rights Governance

Currently, the world continues to face issues of injustice, intolerance, and unrest. Imbalancd, disparate, and unsustainable development persists. The advancement and governance of global human rights faces significant challenges. Humanity urgently needs to explore concepts and solutions for global human rights governance that align with the demands of the times.

The joint pursuit of the BRI conforms to the urgent expectations of many developing countries to promote human rights through cooperative development, assists partner countries in their economic and social development and human rights advancement, and provides new thinking, new impetus, and new opportunities for global human rights governance.

1. Putting people first

People's happy life is the most significant aspect of human rights. Whether the human rights situation in a country is good or not primarily depends on whether the interests of its citizens are effectively safeguarded and whether the people's sense of gain, happiness, and security are enhanced.

The joint pursuit of the BRI adheres to the people-centered thinking of development, focusing on eradicating poverty, increasing employment, and improving people's livelihoods. It aims to ensure that the results of jointly building the "Belt and Road" benefit partner countries' people and make tangible contributions to their economic and social development and human rights advancement. Over the past decade, more than 150 partner countries have embraced the concept of win-win cooperation in jointly pursuing the BRI. They are committed to the cooperative construction of the "Belt and Road" to drive their social and cultural development and to the continuous effort to enhance their people's quality of life and well-being.

Human rights are not privileges enjoyed by some or a few people. Instead, they are the rights enjoyed equally by all. As Stephen Brawer, Chairman of the Belt and Road Institute in Sweden, pointed out, "A crucial concept is achieving the common interests of all." In this sense, the joint pursuit of the BRI aligns with the goals of human rights development and the vision of building a community with a shared future for humanity.

Global human rights governance should adhere to a people-centered approach. The concept of people-centered human rights is rooted in the pursuit of the values of human civilization. It aligns with the UN's original intent to incorporate human rights into the international governance system and promote human rights and fundamental freedoms for all. It respects people's aspirations worldwide for a better life and represents the direction of human rights cause. Therefore, the BRI makes human rights more practical and comprehensive, injecting new meaning into the development of global human rights.

2. Promoting cooperative development

The interdependence and indivisibility of various human rights are fundamental principles of human rights protection. At the same time, for developing countries, which account for over 80% of the global population, the rights to subsistence and development are vital and urgent. Realizing other human rights is difficult or impossible without economic development laying the material foundation and various social conditions. In today's world, where countries' development is deeply intertwined, cooperation and mutual benefit are the best solutions to address development challenges and challenges and obstacles development obstacles. Strengthening cooperation to ensure people's subsistence and development and promoting the progressive protection of other human rights through comprehensive economic and social development holds significant implications for the human rights cause of developing countries and the world.

The Vienna Declaration and Program of Action emphasizes, "The international community should promote an effective international cooperation for the realization of the right to development and the elimination of obstacles to development." The joint pursuit of the BRI has established an inclusive and pragmatic platform for broad international cooperation. Its concept of peaceful cooperation and mutual benefit has attracted the participation of more than three-quarters of the world's countries and over thirty international organizations. Therefore, it can effectively activate the partner countries' economic development potential and promote their economic and social development, thus meeting the practical demand of the international community for "development through cooperation, and human rights through development" and satisfying the needs of the times for advancing the improvement of global human rights governance.

According to Sebastien Perimony, an international affairs expert from the Schiller Institute in France, the joint pursuit of the BRI is not a solo performance by China but rather a symphony of partner countries. China promotes development through cooperation, and the joint pursuit of the BRI has contributed significantly to global development. China's initiative is conducive to achieving win-win cooperation, which is the correct path the world should choose today.

3. Embracing openness and inclusivity

Human rights are historical, concrete, and realistic. Countries have different national conditions, histories, cultures, social systems, and economic and social development levels and face various human rights issues. We should adhere to the principle of universality of human rights and integrate it with the actual situation of each country, follow a human rights development path suitable for each country's national conditions, and determine the priority, ways of protection, and realization methods of human rights based on each country's actual situation. All countries should maintain the diversity of civilizations in a spirit of equality and openness, strengthen dialogue and exchanges among different civilizations, build more consensus through dialogue and exchanges, and jointly promote the development and progress of human rights.

The joint pursuit of the BRI adheres to mutual respect and equal treatment, advocates cultural tolerance, respects the development paths and models chosen independently by each country, respects each other's core interests and major concerns, views the development and policy concepts of other countries objectively and rationally, and strives to seek common ground while reserving differences and working together on development.

An article in the Indonesian newspaper The Jakarta Post points out that the joint pursuit of the BRI spans different countries and regions, diverse cultures and religions, and various customs and lifestyles. In the framework of the cooperative construction of the BRI, the partner countries' common goal is to seek to establish a mutually beneficial partnership.

4. Upholding fairness and justice

Global human rights governance should promote the common values of peace, development, fairness, justice, democracy, and freedom shared by all humans. It should uphold the dignity and rights of people in all countries, promote the building of a community of shared future for humanity, and jointly create a better future for the world. Countries come in different sizes, strengths, and development speeds. Still, they are all equal members of the international community and have the right to equal participation in regional and international affairs, including human rights.

The joint pursuit of the BRI spans different regions, development stages, and civilizations without any sense of superiority toward any. It neither excludes nor targets any party nor imposes any special requirements on the political and economic systems of the partner countries. All BRI partner countries have the right to fair rights, opportunities, and rules as they develop. All BRI partner countries are equal participants, contributors, and beneficiaries, sharing intertwined interests and destinies. The joint pursuit of the BRI upholds the principle of "consultation, contribution, and shared benefits," rejecting the power logic of some countries to conquer or assimilate different cultures and civilizations and striving to promote the construction of fairer and more equitable order and norms.

The development of human rights is a joint endeavor for all humanity. Only by turning "you," "me," and "him" into "us" and ensuring that every country and its people enjoy equal rights and opportunities can the world effectively address global challenges and truly achieve equal participation, cooperation, and shared benefits in the development of human rights.

Conclusion

Though initiated by China, the joint pursuit of the BRI belongs to the world. It is rooted in history and faces the future.

The first decade of jointly pursuing the BRI is one for China and other countries to develop together under a new paradigm of international cooperation. It is also a decade for us to protect and enhance human rights in our common development.

Currently, the world is once again standing at the crossroads of history. Building a community with a shared future for humanity is the future for people of all nations. Only through equality, mutual benefit, cooperation, and shared development among countries can prosperity be sustained and the great dream of every individual thoroughly enjoying human rights be realized.

We believe that in the next decade of jointly pursuing the BRI, China will continue to offer new opportunities to the world through its development, adding fresh momentum to establishing a community with a shared future for humanity. The Chinese people and people of other countries will undoubtedly enjoy broader, more adequate, and more comprehensive rights, achieving all-round development at a higher level.

后 记

　　本书的两份智库报告由中国人权发展基金会和新华社国家高端智库共同组织撰写，中国人权发展基金会副理事长兼秘书长左锋、新华社研究院院长刘刚担任课题组组长，统筹指导撰写、修改、发布等工作。中国人权发展基金会曹蕾、裴闯、胡振家、上官瑶婷、刘浩，新华社班玮、储国强、顾钱江、薛颖、崔峰、刘丽娜、叶书宏、郝薇薇、刘阳、宣力祺、宗巍、李怀岩、梁建强、陈尚营、周蕊、闫睿；杨柳、刘明霞、谢彬彬、张曼、杨德洪、马骁、田栋栋、王玉珏、李洁、贾金明、邓茜、孙萍、韩冰、刘赞、辛俭强、赵晖、卢涛、张健、陈寅、蒋彪、包雪琳、杨天沐、王玉、司源、李良勇、蒋洁、陈霖、蔡施浩、胡柳、余蕊、翟淑睿、赵宇飞、齐健等同志参与报告撰写工作。中央党校（国家行政学院）教授李云龙、中国人民大学法学院教授朱力宇、中国社会科学院国际法研究所副所长柳华文、中国政法大学人权研究院常务副院长张伟、北京师范大学"一带一路"学院执行院长胡必亮、中国社会科学院亚太与全球战略研究院"一带一路"研究室执行主任谢来辉、外交学院人权研究中心主任张爱宁、中国人民大学人权研究中心执行主任陆海娜、副主任李忠夏、武汉大学人权研究院院长张万洪、西南政法大学人权研究院副院长孟庆涛、南开大学人权研究中心副主任唐颖侠、北京理工大学科技人权研究中心执行主任肖君拥、复旦大学人权研究中心研究员陆志安、中国政法大学人权研究院教授孙萌、讲师武文扬、中国社会科学院国际法研究所助理研究员王惠茹、深圳大学中国海外利益研究院助理教授陈思等参与修改工作，在此一并感谢。

　　由于编写水平有限，本书难免存在不完善的地方，敬请读者批评指正。

Afterword

The two think tank reports in the book are written jointly by the China Foundation for Human Rights Development and New China Research (NCR) of Xinhua News Agency. Zuo Feng, Vice Chairman and Secretary-General of China Human Rights Development Foundation, and Liu Gang, Director of the Research Institute of Xinhua News Agency, in the capacity of project team leaders, coordinated and guided the drafting, revising, and publishing work. The comrades from the China Foundation for Human Rights Development who participated in the reports' writing include Cao Lei, Pei Chuang, Hu Zhenjia, Shangguan Yaoting, and Liu Hao. Those from the Xinhua News Agency include Ban Wei, Chu Guoqiang, Gu Qianjiang, Xue Ying, Cui Feng, Liu Lina, Ye Shuhong, Hao Weiwei, Liu Yang, Xuan Liqi, Zong Wei, Li Huaiyan, Liang Jianqiang, Chen Shangying, Zhou Rui, Yan Rui, Yang Liu, Liu Mingxia, Xie Binbin, Zhang Man, Yang Dehong, Ma Xiao, Tian Dongdong, Wang Yujue, Li Jie, Jia Jinming, Deng Qian, Sun Ping, Han Bing, Liu Zan, Xin Jianqiang, Zhao Hui, Lu Tao, Zhang Jian, Chen Yin, Jiang Biao, Bao Xuelin, Yang Tianmu, Wang Yu, Si Yuan, Li Liangyong, Jiang Jie, Chen Lin, Cai Shihao, Hu

Liu, Yu Rui, Zhai Shurui, Zhao Yufei, and Qi Jian. Those participating in the editing include Li Yunlong, Professor of the Central Party School of the CPC (National Academy of Governance); Zhu Liyu, Professor of the Law School of Renmin University of China; Liu Huawen, Deputy Director of the Institute of International Law at the Chinese Academy of Social Sciences; Zhang Wei, Executive Vice Director of the Institute for Human Rights of China University of Political Science and Law; Hu Biliang, Executive Dean of the Belt and Road Institute at Beijing Normal University; Xie Laihui, Executive Director of the Belt and Road Research Institute at the Academy of Asia-Pacific and Global Strategy, Chinese Academy of Social Sciences; Zhang Aining, Director of the Human Rights Research Center at China Foreign Affairs University; Lu Haina, Executive Director, and Li Zhongxia, Deputy Director, of the Human Rights Research Center at Renmin University of China; Zhang Wanhong, Director of the Human Rights Research Institute at Wuhan University; Meng Qingtao, Deputy Director of the Human Rights Research Institute at Southwest University of Political Science and Law; Tang Yingxia, Deputy Director of the Human Rights Research Center at Nankai University; Xiao Junyong, Executive Director of the Science and Technology Human Rights Research Center at Beijing Institute of Technology; Lu Zhi'an, Researcher at the Human Rights Research Center at Fudan University; Sun Meng, Professor, and Wu Wenyang, Lecturer, at the Human Rights Research Institute at China University of Political Science and Law; Wang Huiru, Assistant Researcher at the Institute of International Law, Chinese Academy of Social Sciences; and Chen Si, Assistant Professor at the Institute for China's Overseas Interests, Shenzhen University. We express our gratitude to all mentioned here for their contribution.

Due to limited writing abilities, this book inevitably has imperfections. We welcome readers' criticism and corrections.